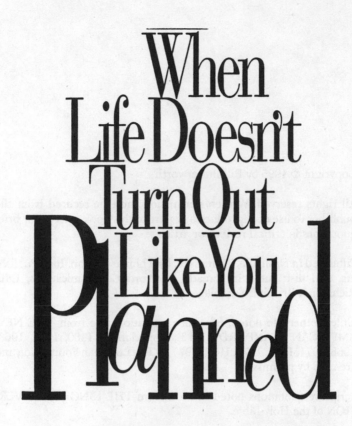

When Life Doesn't Turn Out Like You Planned

Bill Butterworth

A
JANET
THOMA
BOOK

THOMAS NELSON PUBLISHERS
Nashville • Atlanta • London • Vancouver

Published in Nashville, Tennessee, by Thomas Nelson, Inc., Publishers, and distributed in Canada by Word Communications, Ltd., Richmond, British Columbia.

Unless otherwise noted, Scripture quotations are from THE NEW AMERICAN STANDARD BIBLE, Copyright © 1960, 1962, 1963, 1968, 1971, 1972, 1973, 1975, 1977 by The Lockman Foundation and are used by permission.

Scripture quotations noted KJV are from THE KING JAMES VERSION of the Holy Bible.

ISBN 0-7852-7561-4

Printed in the United States of America.

This book is gratefully dedicated to:
Joe Davis
Ed Neuenschwander
Mike Scott
Three of the best friends God could ever give a guy.

CONTENTS

Acknowledgments

There are quite a few people I wish to acknowledge for their contribution to my life in general and this book in particular:

I am deeply indebted to my friends, *Robert and Bobbie Wolgemuth*, for their constant encouragement in my writing pursuits. As my literary agent, Robert has provided fresh ink to a previously dry pen.

It was a crisp winter's morning in Nashville, Tennessee when Robert's partner, *Mike Hyatt* said to me, "You should write a book . . . and you should call it *When Life Doesn't Turn Out Like You Planned*. Thanks for pointing me in the right direction.

I am grateful to all the folks at Thomas Nelson, but especially *Janet Thoma*, for believing in me and believing in this project.

I could never repay what I owe *Mike and Marcia Scott, Joe and Molly Davis*, and *Ron and Kay Nelson*. Thanks for all the phone calls, support, gifts visits, notes of encouragement, and prayers on my behalf. You are *most* special to me.

Ed and Candee Neuenschwander walked this entire journey with me, I am so blessed by God to have this wonderful couple in my life . . . now more than ever.

Thanks to *Ken and Judy Gire* for all the love and encouragement toward getting this story on paper. You are both so sweet.

Gary and Linda Bender . . . thanks for everything,

not the least of which was flying me to Phoenix when you knew I needed it. You are dear friends in my life.

I am still greatly inspired by what I learn everytime I am with *Bill and Denise Bates*. Thanks for allowing God to use you both.

Thanks to *Bob and Barb Ludwig*. Those weekend phone calls from New England always brought hope and encouragement.

I so appreciate *Ken and Marilyn Harrower* and *Rick and Kathy Hicks* for continuing to love me and believing in me even while I was enduring some of my life's darkest days.

So many men at the *Promise Keepers* organization have been so supportive, but most especially two old friends of mine, *Rod Cooper and Glenn Wagner*. Thank you, brothers.

I appreciate men who are very busy in their own ministries, yet took time out to make contact with me to offer encouragement. Thanks to men like *Gary Smalley, Bill Hybels, John Trent, Gary Oliver*, and *Norm Wright*.

Thanks to *Alan Falstreau, Duwaine Ganskie, Fred Sacher*, and *Ken Sheets*. I meet weekly with these four guys and I appreciate the accountability to which they hold me.

This is a book that springs from *my* story, so unlike any other book I have previously written, I have gone to great lengths to *not* talk about my children. but I thank God every day for the love and support I feel from *Joy, Jesse, Jeffrey, John*, and *Joseph*, Thank you all for being so wonderful to me.

Finally, I express deep gratitude to *the Lord* . . . for loving me, for accepting me just the way I am, and for healing me.

PART ONE

Into a Million Pieces

CHAPTer 1

When Your
Life
Meets with
CATASTROPHE

*There are places in the human heart which do not yet exist,
and into them enters suffering that they may have existence.*

—*Leon Bloy*

Attention! Attention! If you are within the sound
of my voice, you are in a danger zone. There
is a hurricane warning for this area. You are being asked to
please evacuate your home immediately, head inland, and
north. I repeat, evacuate immediately, head inland, and
north!

Let's just say it was far from my typical day. I was
in our apartment in south Florida, a twelve-story high-
rise right on the beach. Our apartment was on the
eighth floor, and I remember sitting in my usual position in an overstuffed armchair, tucked behind the
sports section of the *Miami Herald*, when this voice
began penetrating the walls of our tiny apartment. I

rose from my seat to see a Rescue Squad vehicle driving down our street at a very slow speed. The red and blue lights were flashing and its ear-piercing siren was interspersed with a loudspeaker system to attract everyone's attention. But I was still cynical about the whole thing. Why were we being asked to evacuate our home? Wasn't this a little overdramatic? The amplified voice came back over the loudspeaker, as if to answer my questions.

You are in a danger area. Not only is the hurricane imminent, but because of your location right on the ocean, the possibility of a tidal wave is also very great. Please evacuate your homes immediately, go inland, and north!

I looked around and muttered disgustedly to no one in particular, "When you live in Miami, there aren't a lot of other options besides going 'inland and north'!"

But understanding was beginning to dawn. This was no joke. I was staring directly into the face of a natural disaster. I was left with an assignment that would prove to be extremely challenging: Take everything that you ever want to see again, remove it from your apartment, and put it in your small, subcompact car.

At the time this incident took place, there were four of us in our family: me, my wife, Rhonda, our daughter, Joy, and our son, Jesse. My wife brought me back to reality as she started gathering up items of value.

"Okay, okay, everyone stay calm," I announced, more for my benefit than anyone elses. "Rhonda, if we're going to do this right, we need to get organized."

"What do you suggest, Bill?" she asked patiently, yet realizing we really didn't have time to create a "To Do" list for this exercise.

Looking at some of the stuff she had already gathered for the trip, I realized I would have difficulty getting the car filled with what *I* wanted if I didn't get creative, so I quickly suggested a compromise.

"I think we should take turns picking things to put in the car. That way, we can each have possessions we want, and we'll just keep doing that till the car is full."

Rhonda frowned, looking deeply into my eyes, trying to get a read on where I was headed with this line of thinking.

I feared she wasn't going to go with this strategy, so I quickly added, "And since I'm such a gentleman, I'll let *you* have the first pick!"

Anyone who is married can identify with this scene. We were both analyzing every tiny piece of verbal and nonverbal communication. It was a giant, real-life chess game. I was already thinking things like, *Well, I won't pick this particular item, because I know if I don't, she'll pick it later on down the line. I'll pick something she would never pick and that way I'll get both items in the car with us!*

Time was beginning to pass and I hurried her.

5

"Come on, what's your first choice? We need to get moving!"

Once again she looked at me to see if there were any clues to my list of choices. Reluctantly, she uttered her first choice. Looking back, I feel she chose wisely. I was certainly at a place in my life where I would not have made the same decision. She chose . . . *the kids*.

"All right, good choice, Babe!" I cheered her on, clapping and whistling, like she had just guessed the right clue on a TV game show.

"I'm going down to my office to get *my* first choice," I called over my shoulder as I headed for the door. I knew what I wanted. Having just finished graduate school, I had a lot of money invested in books. I wasn't going to leave thousands of dollars in books to float away in the storm.

"What are you getting?" Rhonda inquired.

"Books. I'm getting my complete set of commentaries on 'The Bilingual, Bicuspid Period of Paleozoic Anthropoids in Relation to the Coming Dispensational Holocaust in Quadraphonic Sound.' It's a one-of-a-kind possession. There are only a few of these sets left in the world! It's a smart choice, believe me!"

It was at that point that my usually cool, calm, unflappable wife lost it. She raised her voice to the decibel level of the loudspeaker from the Rescue Squad and replied, "*Books!* We're not filling the car with *books!*" And then she made an executive decision: "You lose your turn!"

Now beginning to mumble, she said, "You made me pick the kids anyway—I really didn't get a first choice." She walked over to our bookshelf in the living room and took some books off the shelf. She turned to me and said, "Books? You want *books?* Well here you go—here are the books we'll take with us!" And with that she handed me a fairly large pile of the most important books in our home. It's probably the same at your place. She chose—*our photo albums.*

Our albums have continued to expand as we have continued to grow as a family. Now, with five kids, our albums are thick. And I'm sure you follow the same pattern we did. You know how it goes:

"Here's a picture of our firstborn, Joy, at birth. Here's Joy at three minutes old. Here she is at one hour old. Here she is on her second day. . . ." Et cetera, et cetera.

Then the second kiddo arrives. "Here's a picture of Jesse at birth. Here he is at two years old!"

Third child: "Here's a shot of our second son, Jeffrey, at birth. Here's Jeffrey at his first day of school!"

Number Four: "Here's John at birth, and here's his school photo from junior high!"

Fifth: "Here's Joseph at birth. . . . [pause] Man, I've got to take some pictures of Joseph!"

I know that sounds horrible, but it's true, isn't it? We've used up so much film on the first kid, we have nothing left for those that follow. I feel sorry for those kids down the line in birth order. They can't even use pictures to prove they grew up in their family! (Unless their mother offers that lame suggestion, "Here you are at your older brother's birthday party—see there? That's your earlobe just at the edge of the photo!")

So, we took what was most important to the Butterworth family—the photo albums. We continued to fill the car and before too long, we were well on our way inland and north.

Well, in His wisdom, God the great Creator and Sustainer saw to it that the hurricane didn't hit our little apartment. For that we were grateful. Interestingly enough, however, God, He of the Master Sense of Humor, saw to it that the hurricane ended up hitting a different area . . . you guessed it . . . inland and north.

We drove right into that sucker. Fortunately, we had the presence of mind to turn the car around and proceed home safely.

I'll come back to this story throughout the book, for it illustrates a variety of issues. But I want to emphasize an important concept that comes from its circumstances. We were far from wealthy people in that small apartment, but we did have some possessions of greater *financial* value than those we took with us. Like so many people who come face-to-face with the issue of survival, we gravitated toward the simple things, the basic things, those things that spoke of our foundation, our roots. An evacuation is not a time to attempt to impress people with an amazing collection of great works of art, rich Asian tapestries, or fine pieces of hand-crafted furniture. No, survival means grabbing albums, pictures, and Granny's quilt that was made just for you.

It has been my experience that when I am in a disastrous time in my life, I'm not looking for the deep secrets of life. I'm looking for the simple, basic truths that will ultimately bring the level of understanding that God intended for me as a result of this experience.

THE TWISTER

After the hurricane, we felt we should relocate to an area less likely to encounter natural disasters. Being pretty perceptive about things of this nature, I moved my family to southern California. And sure enough, we no longer experienced hurricanes. We were a little more susceptible to earthquakes, mud-slides, fire, rain, drought, and winds, but no hurricanes.

So, as an experienced 'Cane and 'Quake man, I had no idea how shook I would be when I encountered my first tornado.

It was March of 1990 and I was the guest speaker at a meeting in Wichita, Kansas. The evening session was to be held downtown at the community center and we all anticipated that it would be well attended. I was stretched out on the bed in my hotel room a few hours before the meeting, when I absentmindedly flipped on the TV, simply to keep me company for a few minutes. Every station had preempted its regular program in favor of the local weather person. *This is not a good sign,* I remember thinking, even before I knew the severity of the situation.

"Yeah, folks, it's a twister all right, and it's headed straight for Wichita. So remember, take the full precautions necessary and hopefully, nobody will get hurt."

I sat in stunned silence. I hit the mute button and picked up the phone to call my host. When he answered, he seemed to sense what was on my mind. "Heard about the twister?" He spoke in the same tone in which he would ask me if I had heard about the latest political joke going around town. It was not at all soothing to me.

"Yes, I just saw the story on the TV news," I replied. "Does this mean we'll be canceling tonight's meeting?" I sat on the bed, fingers crossed, legs crossed, toes crossed, hoping to hear the right response.

"Nah, don't let that little old weatherman bother you." He maintained this unbelievable level of bravado. "More than likely it won't even touch down. Don't worry your little ol' head about it. Just be at the community center at 6 P.M., like we've planned all along. Trust me . . . it'll be great!"

Then he added, "We've still got a little time—why don't you try to catch a little nap before we meet? I bet you'll feel better."

I thanked him for his concern, hung up the phone, and wondered why I had to be in Kansas. Why couldn't I be back in California where the only problem was that the earth moved under your feet?

I showered, dressed, and walked to my rental car in the hotel parking lot. It was so calm outside—too calm. It was that eerie kind of quiet signaling something is rotten in Wichita. Once on the road, I switched on the radio only to discover that all the stations had been taken over by the Emergency Broadcast System. The same message kept being repeated. *If you are in your house, go down to the basement or the safest place possible. For those of you who are in a car right now, please, for your own safety, stop the car on the side of the road, get out of the car, and lie face down in the ditch. Please do not continue driving. You are in great danger.*

I kept switching stations, hoping the one I had just heard was some sort of sci-fi radio experiment, but, unfortunately, they were all saying the same thing. My feeling of absolute panic was further complicated by the fact that *no one* was stopping his car and getting out into the ditch. They were all driving along as if this were a day to enjoy a picnic supper at the lake.

11

"No one else is stopping," I mumbled. "Should I listen to the radio or should I just go along with all the locals?"

Being a man of high integrity, I completely folded to the pressure of those around me. "If they aren't stopping, I'm certainly not gonna stop and look like some out-of-town tourist [which I was] by flopping face-down into a ditch!"

That decision made the ride seem like an eternity. I had this recurring picture of my white, subcompact rental car getting caught in the high winds, flipping over, and spinning around and around. I could imagine myself horribly dizzy, holding my tiny dog, Toto, and screaming, like Dorothy, from the spinning car, "I guess I'm not in Kansas anymore!"

Well, I finally arrived at the community center and to my absolute amazement, there was a wonderful crowd. I gave them the best speech I could under the circumstances. It wasn't until it was over that we realized that the tornado *had* touched down, just north of the city in a little town called Hesston.

I said my thank-yous and good-byes and hit the road back to my hotel. That night, as I dozed off in a fitful sleep, all I could think of was how grateful I would be to fly home in the morning.

About five minutes after one in the morning, the phone rang. Half asleep, I answered it, and it was a familiar voice. "Dad? Are you okay?" It was one of my boys. He had just heard of the tornado on the eleven o'clock news on the West Coast and he was concerned about me. "Dad, I was so afraid you were dead." And with that his voice trailed off.

I assured him of my safety and my love. Promising to see him the next day, I hung up.

I didn't sleep a wink the rest of the night. To think that my boy would be so concerned about his old man is a story that still puts a little lump in my throat. I felt grateful to avoid a catastrophe in that natural disaster. But another one was on its way—and this one would touch down and hit me dead-on.

MY PERSONAL CATASTROPHE

For years and years I have talked about going through crisis situations. But I always spoke as an outsider. A few years ago, however, God, in His infinite wisdom, allowed me to come through a natural disaster of a different kind—a situation that made me a card-carrying catastrophe-endurer.

After eight years as a professor at a Christian college, six years as a counselor, five years as a full-time speaker on predominantly family issues, and seventeen years of marriage, my wife said that our relationship had come to a point of "needed transformation," and in the spring of 1993 she filed for divorce.

I was devastated. All those years I had worked to establish myself as a resource person for "marriage and family" relationships! I had written a number of books, including *The Peanut Butter Family* series, which came out in the eighties, as well as speaking at couples' retreats, marriage conferences, family life seminars, and parenting sessions. It was all going down the drain, along with the most precious human relationship I had ever experienced.

Much later I asked her to clarify her reasoning. She said, "You needed our relationship to stay the same, but I needed our relationship to transform. We were both firm in our points of view. Although neither of us condones divorce, we were not able to survive our differences."

Knowing her as well as I do, I knew that once she made this decision, she would move on and not look back.

I want to be clear, though, that this is not about her, but about *me*. I wish to say nothing that will mar Rhonda's integrity. I am not condoning what has happened in my life, nor am I saying that the pain is gone now and I'm "all better." But the truth is, this is my life now, like it or not.

This was the first time I had to admit my life was not turning out the way I had planned. I felt as if this crisis was like a double-barreled shotgun fixing me in its sights. Not only did I lose the most important human relationship I ever had, I also lost my job. I voluntarily took myself off the speaking circuit entirely, feeling it was the only thing I could do with any shred of integrity since I was speaking about marriage and family. I was virtually out of work for over six months, yet still responsible for the care and feeding of five great kids.

I went through some very real emotions and I am learning some valuable principles that have surfaced in my road to recovery. And be assured, I am still learning, every day.

A RUNAWAY CHILD

That crisis, to me, illustrates what might have occurred in your life as well. Your catastrophe, however, may not have been in the marital realm. Maybe yours is more like the trauma Brent and Elizabeth had to endure. These two are the kind of folks you warm up to immediately. Brent's blue eyes give him a Paul Newman handsomeness and Elizabeth's winning smile could land her on the cover of any major fashion magazine. Besides that, they are humble, gracious, and always willing to serve any way they can.

They have three wonderful children, Michelle, their oldest, and two boys, Martin and Michael. Their family is the all-American dream—solid, sensitive, and positive.

That's why Brent's words threw me for such a curve. He had heard through the grapevine about my crisis and called from his home back East to see if he could encourage me. As he provided me an outlet to pour out my feelings of hurt, despair, and failure, he seemed to identify with every one of them. Finally I just had to ask, "Brent, you seem to be tracking with every emotion I identify. How can you be *that* tuned in to what I am saying?"

His voice choked as he slowly spoke in emotional tones. "Bill, Elizabeth and I have been going through a similar circumstance." He paused, regained a measure of composure, and continued.

"Our marriage is fine, better than ever actually . . . but . . . it's Michelle. She has always been just the sweetest little girl. But adolescence was difficult for her. She got in with the wrong crowd. They really messed with her mind. She started doing hard drugs, smoking, drinking, and sleeping around. All this at sixteen. Can you believe it?" He sighed. He needed another moment of silence.

Then he continued, "She's continued to follow that path. You wouldn't know her if you saw her today." He stopped again, finally blurting out, "She broke our hearts." He sobbed uncontrollably over the phone for another ten minutes.

They had done a good job raising this girl—actually an excellent job. But everything changed.

A BUSINESS FAILURE

Everything changed for Frank when his business took a detour off the road to success. I've always liked

Frank, who's a wonderful blend of go-getter and people person. I wasn't alone in that assessment, either. Frank had risen in the vocational world by using his gifts of business acumen and uncanny people skills. Having a healthy entrepreneurial spirit in him, he ventured out on his own early in life. Everything he touched turned to gold.

Yet, when the economy took a dip, it had a severe effect on Frank's particular business and he was forced to close down.

"I'll never forget when the people came in those big trucks to repossess our office furniture," he recalled. "I sat on the floor of an office once lush and alive, now naked and ashamed. I placed one last call to the person who could turn this whole situation around by granting us a little more time to make good on our loans. He said no. He said he was sorry, but time was up.

"I went out and told the few remaining employees the bad news. I remember one guy just came right up to me, put his arms around me, hugged me hard, and wept like a child. I wept right along with him. This wasn't what I had planned."

SUBSTANCE ABUSE

When Jack and Vicki got married, she had no idea her life was going to turn in an ominous direction. They married young, had two beautiful kids, attended church faithfully, bought the little track home in the suburbs. Jack's life filled with stress, however, because of increasing demands at his job. He began stopping off at a local bar on the way home from work every night in order to "unwind." Gradually, it took longer and longer for Jack to unwind, and it wasn't too long after that Jack started coming home drunk. Vicki became frightened for the safety of her and her two little ones. Jack was different when he was drunk. His kindness was replaced by a mean streak that expressed itself in cutting remarks about anything he could think of relating to Vicki and the girls. She knew it wouldn't take much to move from verbal abuse to physical abuse.

"It was so hard to leave him," Vicki remembers. "He absolutely refused to leave the house, so I had to take the girls and rent a tiny studio apartment. We were so cramped, but at least we were safe.

"I cried myself to sleep every night for six months," she continued. "I couldn't figure out why this had happened to me. This sort of thing happened to other women, not me. It just wasn't what I had planned."

DEATH

The Andersons experienced the same feelings. Cal and Nancy had four boys, all athletes with real futures. Everyone talked fondly of the Anderson boys, with their rugged good looks and pleasing personalities. "Those Anderson boys will go a long way in this world," the townsfolk would say to each other. The oldest boy, Cory, was especially gifted as a baseball pitcher. As a senior in high school, he was already receiving attention from major-league clubs and the scouts made it appear that a contract was virtually locked up.

When Cal and Nancy were awakened from a sound sleep by the ringing phone at 2:30 A.M., both were afraid it could be bad news. It was the local police. "Cory was in an automobile accident. He was not the driver, but he was seriously injured. Another car ran a traffic light and plowed right into the side of the car that Cory occupied. Please come to the hospital immediately."

They drove to the hospital in total silence. Cal and Nancy were too overwhelmed to even speak to one another, so they were two soul mates in prayer, begging God for a miracle.

"We never got to say good-bye to him," Nancy later said. "His head injuries were so massive and severe that he died before we could get to the hospital. There was so much that we never were able to say."

"It was so senseless," Cal added. "He was such a good boy. He had so many little kids that looked up to him—and just like that, it was all taken away."

Nancy said, "You know, it took a long time for us to get on with our lives. We took Cory's death very hard—like it was our own. It paralyzed us for the longest time. It just wasn't the way we had planned our lives to turn out."

BAD INVESTMENTS

No one worked a deal better than Stu. Always dressed impeccably, his fashion statement was one of confidence, poise, and power. Part of Stu's mystique was that he was a keen investor without ever going too far out on the limb. Somehow he was able to bring an even greater return than any of his peers could predict. Stu was one sharp cookie.

That's why one bad investment ruined Stu. He had become so confident over the years; he checked all his bases, double-checked, and then moved ahead with the tenacity of a pit bull. This method had worked well for him over the years. Sure, he was investing a very large amount of money, but, hey, his system never failed. Stu was completely blindsided.

"This investment was so bad, there was no way out," Stu recollects. "I had known other folks who got into a similar situation, but I really felt invincible. So when I lost this money, I lost my shirt—I mean it—I lost everything.

"It was so humiliating to have to go home and tell Sheila and the kids. Debbie cried and little Stu started walking around the house saying, 'We have no money, we have no money.' It was just a four-year-old talking, but it stung like acid in my veins. I became so despondent, I didn't want to live anymore. I'm not proud to admit that I seriously entertained the thought of suicide on several occasions, but it does give you a glimpse into the despair I was experiencing. I lost everything I had worked to accrue all those years."

LIVING ALONE

Maybe you haven't been visited by a life-changing crisis, but you can still relate to the nagging sense of disappointment that comes from reaching a point in life where things haven't turned out like you thought they would.

Dianne knows the pain disappointment brings. She just turned thirty and took it a little harder than most of her friends. The main dilemma in Dianne's life was her fiancé, Paul. They had been dating on and off for almost seven years, and there was a weakness in their relationship that really bothered Dianne. "It was the same old story," Dianne began. "Put quite simply, Paul was unwilling to commit."

Dianne sighed and brushed her bangs away from her deep brown eyes. She is an attractive young woman, certainly not undesirable. She has a contagious smile, an energetic disposition, and a fun-loving personality.

"I really thought Paul was the right guy for me from the time we met back in the mid-eighties. I enjoyed being with him, he was really cute, and he seemed to have his priorities and values really nailed down. I respected him a lot and we got along just about perfectly.

"But the longer we dated, the more I noticed his nervousness about the commitment a marriage would involve. We talked seriously about breaking up and ended up doing just that for about a month." Dianne's body language started to stiffen at this point. She looked off in the distance, then decided to push on.

"After being broken up for a month, Paul decided we needed to be together, so he not only asked me to get back together with him, he brought a diamond ring along with him. He proposed in such a romantic way, I couldn't say no. We set a six-month engagement and began planning a June wedding.

"I was so happy. All my friends were thrilled for me. My mother was the only one who seemed somewhat hesitant about all this. I think her intuitive nature had a fairly good read on Paul."

Dianne's eyes welled up at this point of the story. As she began speaking, it was easy to see why. "By the middle of May, Paul was starting to get some serious cold feet. We talked, argued, cried, and pleaded with each other. But within two weeks, Paul announced to me that he couldn't go through with the marriage. He said stuff like, 'I know this is painful, but at least a broken engagement is better than a broken marriage.'

"I was crushed. I told him I never wanted to see

him again, and I meant it . . . for about two months. By the middle of August I was taking his calls and I finally agreed to start dating him again.

"It got really crazy," Dianne admitted. "Deep down inside I knew this was going nowhere, but I clung to the hope that Paul would somehow change. He didn't. We talked about marriage, but he started clamming up again."

As Dianne paused, it was easy to see how painful this relationship had been on her. "I just told Paul good-bye for the last time. I'm thirty years old and I'm tired of being on the end of this yo-yo."

SHATTERED DREAMS

It's quite possible that you find yourself thinking, *I share the end result of disappointment with all these folks in the stories, but it has nothing whatsoever to do with a crisis of major magnitude. I'm healthy, my marriage is strong, I've got good kids, the business is fine, no major issues assaulting our family right now. But life still didn't turn out as I planned!*

When little things add up to create disappointment, it hurts and the pain is real—no matter what anyone else may say.

Robby is a friend of mine who is an illustration of this type of person. I've known him for a long time and I've watched his life unfold in a very different direction

than he planned back when we were in college together.

We'd sit in the snack shop on campus and pass
hours drinking milk shakes and sharing our dreams
for the future. Robby was a gifted communicator and
his plan was to head toward a career in teaching. I
watched him reach out to high-school kids in particular. He was like a magnet in drawing in those kids to
whatever he was discussing. He was a role model in the
making. Robby was the kind of guy mothers wanted
their sons to be like and their daughters to marry.

Robby's choice for his mate was his sweetheart from
back in high school. He and Pam had been in love for
years and once they graduated, they married a month
later. It was during their first summer together that
Pam's older brother called and asked if Robby would
consider coming back home and taking a position with
his company. Robby was flattered but had already
applied and been accepted in graduate school. His
teaching career awaited the master's degree in educa-
tion that was only a year or two away.

"Looking back, it was a time of real personal un-
rest," Robby now recalls. "No one was putting any
pressure on me toward any particular direction, but I
began feeling an increasing sense that I should take
the job with Pam's brother. I don't know if it was an
inflated sense of family loyalty or what, but before

school opened that fall, I was back home, learning the ropes of the business world with my brother-in-law."

Robby was a natural for his position and he reaped the benefits both financially and emotionally. "It felt good to be told by others around you, 'I don't think this little company would survive without you, Rob!' The paychecks were providing great fun for me and Pam and our new little girl, Cindy.

"My twenties and thirties were a blur of business contacts, conventions, sales seminars, and one client after another. We were at the top of our field, respected by all, even envied by many of our competitors.

"Then, I hit forty. It was the weirdest thing, because all the stuff that had made us so happy for the past seventeen years now seemed empty. Pam thought I was having some sort of breakdown, so she encouraged me to go see a counselor. Through our pastor, I was referred to an excellent therapist.

"It was through his probing questions about my life, past and present, that I came to realize the burning issue behind all this emotion: Deep down inside, I still longed to be that high-school teacher I used to dream about!

"The more we talked, the more I realized that was it. I also came to realize that unlike many guys my age, I really wasn't in a position to walk away from everything in order to go get my degree. People with whom I shared this told me to quit and go after my dream.

That made it increasingly difficult, because nobody understood the fact that I had to continue with my current job. It wasn't my plan to be a forty-four-year-old rookie high-school teacher. It became very clear to me that I was to remain in my business position.

"But that was a hard thing to accept. I remember all the daydreams I had about helping kids. Sure, Pam and I volunteer at our church, working with the high-school kids, but it was a pretty big thing for me to realize that I was not going to be the teacher I had always thought I would be.

"Lots of people look at my situation and say I'm better off where I am. I understand what they mean, but I'm not sure I would agree."

LIFE CAN STINK

Everywhere we turn, we see people facing a time in their journey when they realize life is not turning out the way they planned. "This is it?" they cry with incredulity. "I've worked this hard, remained faithful all these years, played by the rules all this time, and it's not going to happen?" And of course, by "it" they mean the culmination of all their dreams in a happily-ever-after scenario.

Life is cruel, yet no one sets his or her goals and dreams based around that premise. Hope springs eternal, and so we believe we can beat the odds that defeated so many other good folks. Yet, more often than not, even the best of us are struck with the bitter darts of disappointment.

As I began my personal road back to reality, I began encountering people of all makes and models who have survived similar white water. Their tales of going from the agony of despair to the even keel of life again truly inspired me. And it was stories like theirs that gave me the hope that I needed, for, in my own little world, all hope was gone.

Today I am at the place where the words of my story can make their way to these pages. I have learned a great deal, mostly by listening to those who have gone on this road before me. There is a series of principles that most of us who have faced this sort of disappointment glean together. As this book unfolds, I will present many of those principles.

So, if you have been struck by catastrophe, as dark as it may appear, there is room for hope. Be encouraged.

Or maybe you've never felt the water damage of a horrible hurricane or flood, but perhaps you've had to deal with the drip, drip, dripping of a leaky faucet—for over thirty years! It's the same result. And for you, too, there is hope.

PARt TWO

Picking up
the
Pieces

CHAPT*er* 2

Go with the
FLOW

Far better is it to dare mighty things, to win glorious triumphs, even though checkered by failure, than to take rank with those poor spirits who neither enjoy much nor suffer much because they live in the gray twilight that knows neither victory nor defeat.

—*Theodore Roosevelt*

I went to public school back in the old days. If you ask me, things were simpler then. I remember when I was in junior high, all the junior highs were the same. It was before the days of middle schools, intermediate schools, and expando-junior highs. Seventh and eighth grade, pure and simple.

Things were also blatantly sexist back then as well. Remember the days of boys taking shop and girls taking home ec? Apparently the lesson we have learned over the last few decades is that it is just as important that my sons know how to cook as it is for my daughter to know how to weld.

Our junior high required boys to take wood shop in seventh grade in preparation for *heavy metal* . . . eighth-grade metal shop. In our particular school the metal-shop teacher had a reputation that preceded him. He was a complete incompetent. (I should add here that the following story represents the exception, not the rule, concerning metal-shop teachers. If you are a metal-shop teacher, or related to one, believe me, I feel that metal-shop teachers are the salt of the earth.)

No one really knew how this teacher got his job. He was very old, leading to the rumor that he was hired because he had been around at the creation of metal. He rarely stayed in class, choosing rather to get things going and then conveniently disappear to the faculty lounge for a smoke. His sporadic attendance coincided with a rather free-thinking grading policy. Stated simply, you had the entire semester to make *one* metal-shop project. This meant that based on that one contribution, you would pass or fail, sink or swim, live or die.

Another rite of passage regarding metal shop was the time-honored custom of the graduating eighth-grade boys passing on to the incoming eighth-grade boys a list of metal-shop projects that could be constructed in one week or less. Once in possession of this list, a fourteen-year-old had the weight of the world lifted from his shoulders. He could goof off for the entire semester, save the last week for a quickly thrown together metal shop's equivalent to wood shop's spice rack and *bingo*! You have got yourself an "A."

Now, I've never thought of myself as a daring soul, but apparently in those days I had stronger tendencies to push the envelope than I do today. I remember I wasted the entire semester, fooling around, making people laugh, working on my ultimate school triumph—being named the class clown. I even flirted with danger, disobeying many of the safety posters that hung in a typical junior-high shop in the '60s. It's a wonder I didn't incur an injury with this reckless, devil-may-care attitude.

The ultimate expression of my flippancy was how I handled my project. Rather than waiting until the last week, like the rest of my class, I chose to laugh in the face of danger and wait until *the last day* to begin my project.

My faithful list assured me that the easiest metal-shop project to make was a screwdriver. According to the instructions, you simply:

1. Hacksaw a steel rod to the proper length for your tool.
2. Place the rod into the fire.
3. Wait for it to become redhot.
4. Place the red-hot steel on an anvil.
5. Gather a group of guys around you to hum "The Anvil Chorus."
6. Pound the red-hot end of the rod with a mallet, creating the screwdriver tip.
7. Cut a handle out of the yellow handle material.
8. Drill a hole in the handle's center.
9. Place the rod into the handle.

Once it cools and dries—*ta da*! Screwdriver!

I followed the instructions explicitly. I cut the rod, placed it in the fire, let it get redhot, transferred it over to the anvil, gathered the guys around to break into song, and proceeded to hit the red-hot end with the mallet. This is where I got into trouble.

At the time, I thought the problem was my brute strength, but the reality was that I didn't figure on how soft red-hot steel could get. So, when I hit the rod with my mallet, the very first blow flattened a very large area of the rod. I nervously turned and looked at the clock. There was not enough time to start over. I was stuck with this piece of too-flat steel. I turned it over and hammered on the other side, flattening it to an equal distance with the first side. The more I worked on this project, the less it looked like a screwdriver.

In total frustration, I went over to the storage bins and picked out a piece of yellow plastic for the handle. I continued to follow the directions and, if I do say so myself, I made a wonderful handle for an ugly screwdriver. I put the two pieces together and let them cool and dry. I had hopes that once it was cool and dry, it would somehow miraculously transform into a tool like one you'd find at Sears or in your dad's stocking at Christmas.

No such luck. Even cool and dry, it was a hideous metal-shop project. I was angry, upset, and utterly ashamed.

I remember going home that day and replaying over and over a picture of me, next year, in ninth grade, at the high school. I was doing well in all my classes—but every day I was beckoned over the school intercom to catch the bus to take me back over to the junior high . . . to repeat eighth-grade metal shop.

"I just can't flunk," I recall saying to myself. But it was a little too late for internal resolve. I was in deep grease and I knew it.

The next day was the last day of the semester. There was a sense of anticipation in the metal-shop class. A rumor was floating around that the teacher was actually going to make a guest appearance, so we all sat dutifully at our workstations with our semester projects proudly in front of us. Well, the rest of the guys had proud projects; mine, on the other hand was looking worse today than it did yesterday. It was akin to sitting at my workstation buck naked. Either way, it wasn't a pretty picture.

Suddenly the rumor became a reality as the metal-shop teacher somehow found the location of his classroom and paid us all a special visit. He marched proudly up and down the aisles, the smell of stale cigarette smoke wafting through the shop. Sometimes he would nod approvingly, flashing a yellow-stained toothy grin, sometimes he would just walk right by you. Eventually he ended up at the front of the room. He cleared his four-pack-a-day throat and began his impromptu speech:

"Gentlemen, as you know, I have taught metal shop for many, many years." He then paused for maximum effect. "And, as you know, I have seen shop projects come and I have seen shop projects go." He paused again, scanning a room full of eighth graders as if this were a military squadron about to go out on a mission to save the world.

"In all the years I have taught metal shop I have never, ever seen anything like the metal-shop project of—Mr. Butterworth."

All eyes turned my direction.

"Mr. Butterworth, please come up here with me," he beckoned. I had no choice but to comply.

At that point my metal-shop teacher went off on a speech filled with sarcasm and cynicism. He never really put my screwdriver down but rather kept using words like "amazing" and "one-of-a-kind."

I found myself thinking, *Where did this man get his teaching degree? Who certified this guy?* It was like he was a disciple of Don Rickles.

I was horribly uncomfortable, standing up there next to this living legend. Occasionally, he would reach out and put his arm around me, which I concluded was his way of ensuring that I wouldn't run away. Whenever he did this, I felt nauseous, because he didn't smell all that good.

When the speech was finally over, I could barely stand it any more. But his final remarks still ring in my ears to this day.

"So, gentlemen, in conclusion, it is my pleasure to present the award for the Outstanding Metal-Shop Project of the Year to *Mr. Butterworth* . . . for his *chisel*!"

I stood in stunned silence for a split second. But it was in that second that I learned one of the most valuable lessons ever . . . *go with the flow*!

My countenance changed from paralyzed panic to confident charisma. I opened my mouth and put together a little acceptance speech worthy of Oscar consideration. I thanked my mom, my dad, my agent, my producer, and all the little people behind the scenes, without whom this award would not be possible.

It was at this point that one of my classmates tried to yell out, "It's not a chisel—it's a screw—"

I cut him off before he was able to implicate me, thanking everyone for the beautiful award and making my way to the awaiting limo.

Have you ever wondered why God allows you to experience some of the things you go through? I must admit I have always wondered why He would allow me to make a screwdriver that would turn into an award-winning chisel.

LIFE'S CHISELS

After my chisel experience it never even occurred to me that life wouldn't go according to *my* master plan. Wonderful wife, beautiful kids, rising career, financial security . . . it was one fine-looking screwdriver.

And my life didn't fall apart at age forty, either! No predictable, stereotypical crisis of identity at the end of one decade and the beginning of another—no way.

I had my own timetable. My crisis didn't hit till I was forty-one.

I learned "go with the flow" in metal shop, but I had not yet learned how to apply this principle to my life as an adult. Besides the rather obvious pain involved in the ending of my marriage, I was facing a serious vocational dilemma. The decision to take myself off the speaking circuit was both a mark of integrity and a blow to our family's economic survival.

To further complicate matters, my finances continued their downward spiral for well over six months, with no real hint of any rescue. Fortunately, I was able to secure a loan to keep the family afloat, but of course, it would create a tidy sum to be placed in the category of "debt."

I was not yet understanding how to go with the flow. I was frantically trying to make something happen in the job market, sending résumés and applications to a wide variety of institutions—most of which I would never have fit in with anyway. But like I said, I was utterly down and desperate.

What I was to learn was that God was teaching me to go with the flow. He had a plan much more profound than anything a panicked, middle-aged guy could orchestrate. And now, going with the flow has given me a new lease on life. Here's a portion of the story to show how this occurred:

A man I had known on a more casual basis over the last ten years was to come back into my life in a major way. Through his love, friendship, and good business sense, he was God's tool to begin putting the shine on my chisel.

I had written three books over the decade of the eighties, and I had always fancied myself something of a writer. But I had allowed my writing craft to sit on the workbench untouched for years, while I pursued my speaking career with a greater passion and fire. Another good friend (whom I'll tell you about in greater detail later in the book) suggested that I contact Robert Wolgemuth, who was then (and is now) a literary agent. My friend encouraged me to use my writing gifts and appealed to my common sense, explaining to me how I could work out of my home. *I could stay around for my kids and I could also kinda keep to myself until I'm really ready to face the world again*, I thought. So I called my old friend, Robert. With that, going with the flow was beginning.

"I don't have anything I really want to say in a book of my own at this point," I began cautiously over the phone with Robert. "But a friend of mine thought I might be able to get some ghostwriting assignments or work-for-hire types of projects. Do you think this idea has any merit?"

Robert agreed with my friend and started working on my behalf immediately. It was hard for a guy like me to believe what would happened. I had never been all that high on any kind of agent, thinking they were often more trouble than they were worth, but I was to turn 180 degrees with Robert.

He understood how urgently I needed work, and thus, he had me a full ghostwriting book contract within *one week* of my signing on as a client of his.

The project went well and each day I seemed to have a little more excitement about my newfound profession. Sure, I missed the speaking circuit, but this was a great way to continue communicating without ever leaving my home and without anyone knowing it was me!

By February 1994, Robert began looking for another project for me. He casually mentioned on the phone one day that one of the Dallas Cowboys, Bill Bates, was thinking of writing his autobiography. Bill was in the market for a writer who could capture his thoughts on paper.

"Would you be interested in this project?" Robert inquired over the phone.

"Would I?" I replied. "Absolutely!"

"Okay, let me see what I can do."

The Cowboys had just won their second Super Bowl in a row and the off-season was a little more hectic for their team than for some of the others in the NFL. I waited and prayed and waited and prayed. Finally Robert called with some news.

"Bill seems interested in working with you, but before he signs an agreement, he would like to meet you in person."

I felt this was a reasonable request and agreed to meet Bill at his earliest convenience, since my schedule was wide open.

"Well, that's where it gets a little tricky," Robert said. "Bill is on an amazing schedule, even now in the off-season. He was wondering if you could meet with him for a couple of days next week."

"That's no problem at all, Robert," I replied. "I'm not all that in-demand right now," I added, in a small attempt at out-of-a-job humor.

"I know, but that's all going to change," Robert reminded me in his usual encouraging style.

"So does Bill want to come out here to California, or does he want me to visit him in Dallas?" I asked.

"Well, neither," Robert replied. "He's receiving an award next week and that looks like the only time and place he can meet with you. So, if you're ready for this, friend, you are on your way to Baltimore."

"Baltimore?"

"Yep. Bill's receiving the Ed Block Courage Award at a black-tie dinner there. Pack your tuxedo, buddy, you're entering a whole new world."

And with that phone call I came one step closer to understanding "go with the flow." I could have never orchestrated this alliance—I just needed to accept where I was, and move with it.

NEVER GIVE UP

Flying to Baltimore, I had no idea what to expect from Bill Bates. In the past fifteen years I had spoken to almost all the teams in the National Football League and many of the major-league baseball teams, so I knew a little about professional athletes. Some were good and they knew it, others were good, but you'd never know it to be around them. I was praying that Bill would be the latter.

As soon as I met him, I knew God had answered my prayer.

Bill and I hit it off immediately. He was one of the kindest, most thoughtful guys I had ever seen in a pro-athlete context. Like so many pros, he was an animal on the field, but a true gentleman off.

But it was when I went to see him receive his award that I began to see why this guy was suddenly put into my life.

Looking back on that evening, there was a certain

unreal quality to it. There I was, filled with the lingering pain of my crisis, my insides still one large, raw, open wound. Yet on the outside, I was decked out in a handsome, black tuxedo, making my way through an ornate hotel lobby, looking for the driver that Bill had arranged for me so that I could get from the hotel to the banquet. Before long, I was shown to my stretch limo. The driver simply needed to confirm that I was Mr. Butterworth, to which I heartily replied, "Yes, I am!"

"So, Mr. Butterworth, I understand from Mr. Bates that you are a writer," the driver began his required casual conversation with me.

"That's correct."

He sighed and confessed, "My, that sounds like an exciting job. What a wonderful career you have!"

I smiled and nodded, but inside I couldn't help but think, *What? Are you crazy or something? During the last six months my life has gone straight to the toilet and you have the unmitigated audacity to sound envious of me? You don't have a clue how much better off you are in the driver's seat of this limo.*

Once we arrived, I was escorted to the main table where the tuxedoed Bill Bates was already seated. He was flanked by people on his right and left. They were all lined up, waiting for an autograph from him. They had an assortment of Cowboy paraphernalia—jerseys, helmets, balls, trading cards, pictures, and programs.

As he patiently signed each item, the crowd watched him spell out the signature. Not only was the autograph a treasure, but as he signed they got an up close look at the biggest hunk of men's jewelry they may have ever seen . . . a Super Bowl ring.

When the crowd finally subsided, we small-talked at the table. I knew from the start that his was a great story. The little scrappy kid from Tennessee who was overflowing with energy as a boy was considered too small and slow to ever make it in the pros. It was the embodiment of setting your sights on your goal, giving it all you've got, and then achieving it. He made it work, and in doing so, I knew his story would inspire others.

Finally, we got around to the function we were attending. "What's this award all about?" I asked.

Bill smiled his winsome grin and admitted, "This is one of those awards that initially no one wants to win."

"Why's that?" I quizzed.

"Because the Ed Block Courage Award goes to the player on each NFL team who best displays courage in coming back from some sort of major setback, usually an injury," he replied with a laugh.

"So you don't want to get it, because you have to be injured first," I responded.

"Right . . . but once you're hurt, it's the best honor you can receive."

With that I was to hear for the first time the fascinating story of Bill Bates and his ability to go with the flow.

Part of what makes Bill so remarkable is the fact that he is absolutely merciless to his body. Anyone who has ever seen him make a play on the football field knows that he is one of those guys who will sacrifice himself *on every play* to make a tackle. As a result, he has had more than his share of injuries . . . actually over *two dozen* in his college and pro career.

He's had turf toe, torn groin muscles, pulled stomach muscles, thigh bruises, hip-pointers, broken ribs, shoulder separations, broken wrists, two broken thumbs, dislocated pinkies, a broken right ring finger (which makes for a staggering juxtaposition against his Super Bowl ring!), neck stingers, stitches in the neck, lips, chin, and eyes, and a concussion that sent him into La-La Land so seriously that for a while afterward, he kept referring to his wife, Denise, as his girlfriend!

But that banquet in Baltimore was to honor him for coming back from his most severe injury, the tearing of his anterior cruciate ligament (ACL) in his left knee. Normally it is an injury that sidelines you for such a long time, it often ends your career. Bill astounded everyone by coming back to 100 percent the next season!

This was far more than a writing partnership, a work-for-hire agreement. This man was placed right next to me to show me what "go with the flow" looks like in person. There just didn't seem to be an injury that could bring him down.

Once we hit it off in Baltimore, I traveled to Dallas

on numerous occasions to meet his family and interview different people close to him. When I got to know his charming wife, I took her aside and said, "Okay, Denise, give it to me straight. How has Bill been able to come back from setbacks that would've ended other guys' careers?"

Her eyes sparkled as she spoke of Bill. "He refuses to let life get him down. All his life he's had to prove himself, so his injuries were just another dimension of that proving ground. He sticks with it, refuses to get discouraged, takes what is given him, and moves on to make the best of it. He knows the value of the words, 'Never give up.'"

"Make the best of it and never give up," I repeated. That's what made Bill Bates so enduring. Certainly it was never in his plan to be sidelined with injuries. But it didn't stop him . . . he would just go with the flow.

Tom Landry agreed. While interviewing him for the book, I blurted out the obvious question: "How did Bill ever make the team if everyone thought he was too small and too slow?"

The master of the concise answer just looked at me and said it all in one word: "Heart. Nothing was going to keep him from making our team. He proved it over and over again. He made the cut every year and the Cowboys were much better off because of it. Bill Bates is a winner."

Interview after interview revealed the same information. Bill's strength and conditioning coach, Mike Woicik, told me that in all his years as a trainer, he *never* saw anyone come back quicker than Bill Bates. "He sets his mind to accomplish something and then he hauls off and does it!"

What was going on here was obvious. Naturally, a wonderfully inspiring story came to fruition as a result of our time together. *Shoot for the Star* has already challenged thousands of readers to reach for their personal best. But more was happening beyond my gathering of material for the book. I was getting a crash course in a principle of life that I desperately needed to learn. I had spent a long time swimming upstream. I had fought the current from the day my crisis began. I thought I could beat it by paddling against it. But the release was found in giving in to it.

My life was never going to return to the happy little nuclear family it had been in years past. To sit there and resist that notion was a complete waste of time and energy. It was as foolish as it would have been to sit on the sideline and sulk because the ACL in your left knee was never going to be injury-free again.

No, the lesson was: Begin the process of picking yourself up again. It might mean redefining yourself, but that's okay. There was also the distinct possibility that what had happened to me had occurred for my *benefit*. Instead of fighting it, accepting that fact could help me learn why God had chosen to allow this circumstance to occur.

There was something in all this pain that I would not learn were it not for the pain. It was my job to find that lesson and benefit from it.

Watching Bill and Denise Bates taught me something very valuable: It isn't always bad, even though it may look that way.

CONTENTMENT WITH LIFE'S CHISELS

I came face-to-face with a biblical principle I had never needed to wrestle with before. It centered around Paul's words in Philippians: "Not that I speak from want; for I have learned to be content in whatever circumstances I am."[1]

Contentment is a difficult concept to grasp in our hard-driving American culture. We say we're content, but our lifestyles reveal the truth. If we were content, we wouldn't worry like we do. We wouldn't be driven. We wouldn't keep struggling with the same feelings of inadequacy and dissatisfaction.

I talked contentment when things were going well. When my life caved in, I didn't even talk it anymore.

I lived more like the first part of the verse. . . . I lived in *want*. I wanted the old days back; the days of fun and freedom and love and companionship and unity and affection and sunshine and lollipops. . . .

I wanted life to be the screwdriver I had planned

all along that it would be. But God planned a chisel and no matter how loudly I demanded a screwdriver, it never changed back.

Another friend of mine, dealing with his own share of life's disappointments, commented to me, "You know, Bill, the day I accepted that this was the way my life was going to be, my life actually started improving. I didn't make an inch of progress beforehand. I went for months feeling sorry for myself, yearning for the successes of the past, staying absolutely motionless in the river of life. I used up so much energy treading water, I came perilously close to drowning."

He went on, "I wanted that promotion so badly, I went into a funk when it didn't happen. I shut down emotionally to the point that I almost lost the position I had. It would have been horrible to think what would have happened if I had lost my job over this issue. . . . I thought it was difficult going home and telling my wife I didn't get promoted. Imagine what it would have been like to tell her I got canned!"

Like so many others, I am learning what it means to go with the flow. The more I accept what is happening in my life and seek to learn from it, the more progress I make. It would be a bold-faced lie to suggest to you that I no longer have days of yearning for the past. I do. I sometimes feel tremendous longing for the life I had initially planned for myself and my family.

That's not evil, "falling off the wagon," or "regressing into a deeper state." That's real life.

Part of the process of going with the flow involves *time and distance*, which we'll discuss in the next chapter. Try as we might, we can't rush these things. Especially if our crisis throws us into some sort of grief, there are stages that must be gone through before ultimate acceptance is at hand. So don't misread my words; this is not a plea for hurried acceptance, but for more of a quiet resolve to work with the process.

I feel I need to add a word of caution here. As I have been addressing the whole concept of going with the flow, it occurred to me that someone might read this chapter and entertain a serious misconception. What I am referring to is a person who is currently in an abusive situation who might use the idea of go with the flow as justification for staying in a circumstance that is actually dangerous. Don't misread these words, for that is not my intention. You were never meant to endure abuse that is threatening to your welfare. Don't go with the flow—just go.

In my case I make a little more progress in life every day. And part of it is learning the lesson of going with the flow. I'm thankful to God for bringing people into my life who were human illustrations of the truth I needed to see. Because of them, I am learning to be content. I am more at peace. I am not so much in want.

Life is a chisel . . . so don't screw it up.

CHAPTer 3

Time and Distance Provide PERSPECTIVE

The glory is not in never failing, but in rising every time you fail.

—Chinese proverb

When I was going through the trauma of my crisis, I found that the telephone became a real intruder. My desire was to be completely alone, cut off from everyone in the real world, so I could cry, grieve, feel sorry for myself, and oftentimes curl up on the couch in a fetal position.

Thank goodness for answering machines. It was wonderful to have the option of not answering the phone until I had screened the call. Though it was rather rude, I recall only taking calls from people I wanted to at that point of my life. The rest of them went to voice-mail purgatory.

One autumn morning I received a call from a very

good friend of mine, Gary Bender, in Phoenix. Our friendship goes back a long way, yet we both can get so busy that time can slip by us without our realizing it. As I heard his voice on the answering machine I realized we had not spoken since I had become single again. Taking a deep breath, I picked up the phone, automatically stopping the answering machine's tape. "Hi, Gary, I'm here, I'm just screening my calls," I admitted.

"How are you doing?" he asked. "It's been a long time since we've talked. Bring me up to date."

"Well, I hope you're sitting down," I began. "Updating you on how I'm doing may include some surprising news."

And with that I launched into the whole story of my personal catastrophe. Gary was stunned.

"Bill, I had no idea," was about all he could say initially.

"I know, Gary. No one had any idea. I've been doing a pretty good job of keeping everything undercover. I'm just so embarrassed about the whole thing, I don't know any other way to handle it."

As he started to regain his composure he asked me, "So what can Linda and I do for you?"

"Pray," was the only thing I could think of at the time. "And keep being my friend."

"Are you real busy over the next few weeks?" Gary asked in genuine sincerity. When I explained that I was virtually unemployed, he understood I had plenty of time on my hands. "Okay, let me work on something, and I'll get back to you." His comment was a little vague, but I didn't give it much thought at the time.

I was completely surprised when the next day a Federal Express truck delivered a round-trip airline ticket to Phoenix, for the next week!

"What's this all about?" I asked Gary after I speed-dialed his number.

"We want you to come and spend a few days with us," he explained. "Linda and I feel you could use a little change of pace. Linda will be here when you arrive, but she'll be leaving the next day to visit an old friend of hers in Colorado so you and I will have a few days to be a couple of bachelors. I figured we'd play a lot of golf, go out and eat like a couple of pigs, sit around the pool, and just catch up with each other." Gary paused and added, "Please don't turn us down, Bill. I know you'd do the same thing for me if the tables were turned."

So that's how I ended up in Phoenix. We played lots and lots of golf, we went out and ate Mexican one night, big steaks another night, and, as you would expect from a couple of "bachelors," a plateful of barbecue ribs. But there was one activity I hadn't planned on. One night at dinner Gary spontaneously raised an option:

"Hey, I've got a great idea, Bill. Whattya say tomorrow we get up real early and climb Camelback Mountain? Linda and I do that a lot . . . the sunrise is absolutely breathtaking . . . it'll be fun!"

I pondered this request for a second. Gary was a jock and I had the athletic prowess of a doorknob. What he thought to be easy might be a flirt with death for me. But . . . how could I refuse without looking like a complete wuss?

"Sounds like a cool idea!" I gushed, hoping my fake enthusiasm was not a tad overplayed.

The next morning proved to be one of the more amazing in my life.

As promised, we were up before the sun was even close to appearing. On Gary's suggestion, I dressed in a light T-shirt, some loose-fitting shorts, and a pair of hiking boots that he loaned me for our adventure. We drove over to the base of Camelback, hopped out of the car, and set off on our journey. Carrying nothing but water bottles, we followed a trail that Gary had obviously traversed many times before. I had no idea what was in store for me, Mr. Mountain Man.

"Are you going to have any problem climbing?" Gary asked.

"Nah," I replied in utter ignorance. "Don't forget, Gary, I live in the foothills of the Sierra Nevada!" I boasted. "I walk all the time out there!"

It was only a matter of seconds before I would experience the utter lunacy of my last statement. I was to see that the foothills and Camelback are about as similar as putt-putt golf and Pebble Beach.

I was less than ten minutes into the hike when I had my first glimpse of the closeness of death. My thighs were screaming, I was light-headed, my mouth was parched, and I was sweating like mad.

"Are you all right, Bill?" Gary asked as he stopped to attend to me.

"This . . . is . . . harder . . . than . . . I . . . thought. . . it . . . was . . going . . . to . . . be," I choked out in desperate tones.

"We can turn back if you want," Gary immediately responded. We sat in silence for a minute and then he added, "But I know you'll feel really good about yourself if you can hang in and make it all the way to the top."

I looked at him with the saddest look I could produce, but it profited nothing.

"We'll stop as often as you need to . . . but it'll be worth it when you see things from the top, believe me." He had just the right blend of sympathy and motivation, because he convinced me to continue.

We trudged on our way, Gary and I. He was barely out of breath, whereas I needed eight to ten more stops. I had used up all my water fifteen minutes into the climb. I began to envision myself passing out, falling down the side of the mountain, and becoming an awful spectacle for all of those living in the Valley of the Sun. I think I had lost touch with reality, for I began to think of myself as Piggy, the kid who falls off the cliff at the end of the book *Lord of the Flies*. I remembered how his insides spilled out all over the rocks.

What normally took Gary less than an hour took us over two hours. For me it seemed like two decades . . . I was certain I was a grandfather several times over in the time it took me to scale my own Everest. Of course, because of the extra time involved, we were nowhere near the summit when the sun rose. I was in such a crazed mental state, I don't even recall a change from darkness to light.

But once we were on the tip of Camelback's hump, I discovered that Gary was a man of his word. The view was spectacular! In the midst of my exhaustion, I had a sense of exhilaration.

Gary was beaming broadly, reflecting how proud he was that I had accomplished this feat. I was over-come with the feeling that I wanted to do something to make this an occasion I would never forget.

"Gary, would you do me a favor?" I asked as the idea dawned on me. "Would you take a minute and just say a little prayer for me and my kids? It would really make this a special moment."

He nodded and right there, in the midst of God's glorious splendor, a man prayed that his brother would be healed from all the pain he was experiencing.

It really was a short prayer. Nothing eloquent or grandiose. But by the time he said "Amen," I was weeping.

Gary reached over and patted my shoulder. He then held out his water bottle, offering to share his refreshment with me. It was the coldest, clearest water I had ever tasted, or at least that's how it felt at the time.

After a few more moments of rest, we started down the mountain. Going back down was so much easier! Obviously it's easier physically, but I felt recharged inside—mentally, spiritually, and emotionally.

It was remarkable to me that just twenty short minutes before, I had felt I was knocking at death's door, and now, with the advantage of a little time and a little distance, everything was taking on a fuller perspective.

Today, whenever I get back to the Phoenix area and see the Camel's back silhouetted in the distance, I get a feeling of joy and accomplishment. That day has become a lifelong memory.

SEEING THINGS FROM THE TOP

Climbing that mountain was a real-life analogy of what I was going through in day-to-day existence. In the midst of my catastrophe, I was in the early stages of scaling that rock. I was in the same level of pain emotionally; I felt as if my legs were burning to the extent that I thought they would break off. I was to the place where I didn't know if I could go on. But if I could somehow keep climbing to the top, there would be a victory.

The top of the mountain rewarded me with something I would never have seen if I hadn't gone through the pain to get there. Certainly it was a breathtaking view from an all-new perspective. But the mountaintop actually represented a time of rest from the rigors of climbing, and it also represented some distance from the upward march that nearly killed me. Time and distance. They are great healers.

In the language of the psychologist, we are talking about the *process of grieving*. Back in the 1970s Dr. Elisabeth Kübler-Ross researched this issue in depth and out of that study came her stages of grief, which pretty accurately chart the road most folks must travel after they have encountered a loss. I've seen the list in longer versions and shorter versions, but the main elements are these:

- Denial
- Anger
- Depression
- Resolution/Acceptance

Some lists include words such as *bargaining, sadness,* and *forgiveness* as well. These are all important concepts, but it was those other four elements that were most important to me in my journey.

If you've been through rough times lately, this process may look familiar. Our first response is to deny the catastrophe. Deep down we seem to be saying that by denying it we may make it go away. Unfortunately, that is never the case. Turning away from the reality of a situation doesn't put all the pieces together again.

I was pretty good at denial. I could even deny that I was in denial. I remember years ago, early in our marriage, Rhonda would describe me as a person who would "whistle past graveyards." While she was very much a realist, I didn't want to deal with anything harsh, so I would look a different direction, or change the subject, or whistle past this painful side of life.

When my crisis hit, I was to learn "denial is more than a river in Egypt" (one of my favorite one-liners).

I went into hiding. No one outside the immediate family knew the circumstances of my pain. Part of that was embarrassment, but I have come to believe that another part of it was denial. "If I keep this quiet, everything will eventually come back together, and no one will need to know about the difficulties."

But the longer my trauma persisted, the closer I came to the truth. My marriage was over. I then moved into the next stage: anger. I wasn't the type to shake my fist at God, blaming Him for all that was wrong with my world. But I *was* the type to explode in anger at

Rhonda. In my wrath, I would call her on the phone and pop my cork on a regular basis. As I look back on that time, I feel badly for what I said and did. Anger, though a necessary stage in grieving, is an ugly time slot.

I would feel horrible after my phone conversations, so I quickly moved into the third stage: depression. I had heard a clinical definition of depression for years, but now I was experiencing it: anger turned inward. While I struggled with anger, I excelled at depression.

I was virtually useless as a human being. I sat around, moped, felt sorry for myself, cried, lost weight, couldn't sleep, became irritable, and only occasionally mustered up enough strength to go out in the garden and eat worms.

If it wasn't for my friends, my counselor, and the Lord, I may not have made it.

It took me about six months to move through the grieving process to where I was able to come to acceptance and resolution. Even as I write those words I must hasten to add that I am *still* in that process. I wish it were as easy as clicking off these stages, but the truth is we often revisit each and every stage. I still have moments where I can't believe what has happened. I still get angry and depressed. But the large chunks of time occupied by each of those stages appear to have passed.

You need to feel permission to grieve over *any and*

all of the losses you've encountered in life. If you've lost a family member or close friend to death, allow yourself to grieve over that loss. If you've lost a mate to divorce, you'll need to grieve that loss. If your business bottomed-out, let yourself grieve the loss of that business. If your medical report is less than clean, allow yourself to grieve the loss of your health.

In grieving life's losses, we apply the principle of time and distance to bring perspective. We need the days, weeks, and months provided by the grieving process to work through our dilemmas. Our losses were like a swift kick to the stomach, knocking the wind out of us. Grieving gives us the necessary time to catch our emotional breath.

In many cases, grieving not only gives us a second wind, but it also provides us with some essential emotional distance. After years of closeness with a person, place, or thing, we need some refocusing. Distance allows us to shift into the new mode for the future.

Also, as I write about my six-month grieving period I feel compelled to state another very important observation: *Each person's timetable is unique.*

Depending on who you are and what you've been through, your grieving will vary significantly from someone else's. Like so many of life's issues, it's one that demands balance. Working through something too quickly will leave you with unfinished business. Allowing grieving to drag on for an overextended amount of time will prove to be taxing, not only on you, but on those around you.

How short is "too quick" and how long is "overextended"? I don't know, because it truly is a unique calendar for every person. This is where a counselor can provide a valuable service, assisting you in walking through your time and distancing.

When we arrive at acceptance and resolution, we discover that this is also an area of great latitude. There seem to be two general categories that people fall into once they reach acceptance.

HAPPY ENDINGS

Happy endings are the storybook finales. "And they lived happily ever after" is the last thing lots of kids hear each night before they doze off to sleep. Yet in the cynical 1990s, we have dismissed happy endings as pure fiction. They just don't happen, we tell our kids, after reading them two dozen examples.

Realism tells us that it is very unlikely we will live happily ever after. But it is not an impossible dream. Many folks have come back from crisis only to discover a more wonderful life than they experienced previously. There are no guarantees, but it is certainly possible.

Jeannine is a good example. Born and raised in a strict Christian home, she met Danny in seventh grade. They dated all through high school and were married the summer between his freshman and sophomore years in college. They were truly happy for a lot of years.

But Danny always liked to live on the edge, and this bright, young, adventurous Christian man became addicted to cocaine. He tried to quit, but his sober days would be pitifully outnumbered by his high days. He was angry—mostly at himself—but he spent his anger abusing Jeannine, and Reggie and Shawn, the two boys they had parented over the last eight years.

Danny and Jeannine divorced after ten years together. On the outside, Jeannine told her friends how much better life would be without having to live with the potential danger of Danny's violence.

But inside, Jeannine was sick. She felt betrayed, ripped off, and, worst of all, horribly alone. Like so many dutiful men and women of our age, she found a job and resigned herself to raising her two boys with the most dignity she could muster.

Jeannine walked through the grieving process for about nine months. Like me, she battled with the tendencies to fall back into the old ways of thinking, including denial, anger, and depression.

Acceptance and resolution arrived in Jeannine's life at about the same time Dwayne did. It was a totally unscripted, unexpected occurrence: Dwayne Peterson ran into Jeannine while attending a concert at the local community center. They introduced themselves to each other during intermission in the lobby. In an uncharacteristically brave move, Dwayne asked her if she'd like to have dessert with him after the concert. Jeannine agreed and doesn't remember much of the second half of the concert.

They hit it off. He had lost his wife to cancer two years before and through that ordeal had become a Christian, attending the sister church of the one Jeannine was attending. They began dating and before long their attraction to each other grew into a deep love. Dwayne proposed exactly one year later, in the lobby of the community center. A few months later they were married.

"Dwayne is the most loving and caring person I have ever met," Jeannine admits. "He is so sweet to me and the boys. He has his moments like anybody, but the overall effect of being his wife is more than I ever imagined life could be."

Jeannine's life story seems to be moving down the "happily ever after" path, even though the cynics still scoff, saying it'll never last because it's a second marriage for both. Jeannine and Dwayne just might prove their critics wrong.

Harold also seems to be experiencing that happily-ever-after ending. When Harold watched his small company get eaten by a huge business conglomerate, he had no idea how hard it would be. He was in denial for the longest time, and then his anger was lethal.

During that time Harold developed a stomach ulcer. From that point on, he was rarely seen without his trusty bottle of Mylanta®, swigging it like a drunk chugs his whiskey.

The big New York firm that orchestrated the hostile takeover tried to be as accommodating as a heartless business could be. They provided him with a temporary office "for the interim"—while he looked for another position. Every morning, five mornings a week, Harold faithfully arrived at his temporary desk at 6:50. "I wasn't doing anything," he now recalls, "but I was there early just in case there *was* going to be anything to do."

In this transitional period, Harold reacquainted himself with an old friend from business school. Bernie Dodd was a casual acquaintance from the past, but in God's great timing, he and Harold hit it off one day at lunch and the creative wheels started to turn.

"I can't believe you're between jobs right now," Bernie spoke exuberantly over his Caesar salad. "I'm putting together the final puzzle pieces for a business that's tailor-made for you. I really need a CEO. . . . Harold, you've gotta take it!"

Harold went home and carefully reviewed Bernie's business plan. Everything seemed in order and he was right, it was the perfect position for him.

After getting counsel from several close friends,

Harold telephoned Bernie to tell him he'd accept the CEO position of the new company.

Well, the rest, as they say, is history. The company exploded onto the scene, amazing even its biggest supporters. Harold ceaselessly credited Bernie for his vision and leadership, while Bernie put the credit squarely on the shoulders of Harold for his keen management skills and team-building gifts. It was the best of times.

"When the first business was taken from me, I thought seriously of leaving the business world altogether," Harold recalled. "I was going to go into teaching or research or join a monastery, anything to get away from the horrors of business."

"But time heals wounds," he added. "I was an angry man for over a year, but eventually I got past it. And that's when this new deal came up to completely revolutionize my life. God has really blessed me."

Troy is another guy who feels blessed by God. At thirty-three years of age, Troy was a strikingly handsome guy who worked out regularly to keep his body strong and healthy. Always one to watch what he ate, he was a model of good health. His wife, Kay, was equally attractive, and when the two of them walked down the street with their daughter, Hillary, they looked like something out of *People* magazine.

With everything going Troy's way, he was totally

devastated when he was summoned back to his doctor's office after a routine physical.

"I don't want to alarm you," the doctor began, "but I think we need to run a few more tests."

"Why?" Troy asked.

"Let's take the tests first and then I'll answer all your questions," the doctor replied matter-of-factly.

Troy was one nervous dude the next day when he showed up at the local hospital for a battery of tests. The time between the tests and the doctor's call seemed like an eternity. Finally he was told to come to his physician's office.

"Troy, there's no easy way to say this, so I'll just tell you the simple facts. We have discovered a mass in your lymph nodes that is cancerous. We believe we can go in there and get it, but this is not something that has any guarantees with it."

Troy sat motionless. Not hearing anything after the word *cancerous*, he was scheduled for surgery without even realizing it.

"'My life is over,' that's what I remember thinking," Troy said, recalling that moment. "I was so stunned I didn't even cry. I couldn't. It was like my body went into shock. I completely shut down."

But Troy is one of those fortunate individuals whose cancer was caught at an early stage. "They went in there and they got it all," he shared. "Six years have gone by since the surgery, but I go back every six months for a checkup and to this day I am still receiving a clean bill of health. I'm so grateful to God for giving a happy ending to my story."

PEACEFUL ENDINGS

After some time and distance, we eventually come to a place of accepting what has happened to us. We make the necessary adjustments and move on with the new dimensions of our lives.

Not everyone experiences happy endings. But there is another alternative that is desirable: a *peaceful* ending. It's the ending most of us will probably realize. Some people move all the way to happy, but peace is attainable for everyone. I choose the two words, *happy* and *peaceful*, with great care and purpose, for I believe peace is far superior to happiness in the big pictures of our lives.

Allow me to contrast each of the three scenarios above with scenes of different resolve. Despite ending differently, they still end with the realization that what has happened is in God's hand and therefore, good.

Caroline went through the trauma of divorce, like Jeannine. Married for fourteen years, the transition into single life was quite difficult. "I really didn't want to get out there in the dating scene. I was too old for that. I decided to just dig in, work my job, raise my kids as a single mom, and learn to accept my position in life."

"It was real hard at first," she remembered, "but the Lord was very real to me in my times of loneliness and despair. Time really is our friend. Through time, I have come to a place of accepting where I am in life. Sure, if the right man came along, I'd love to remarry. But it's not going to happen in the immediate future, so I have come to the resolution that it's good to be where I am right now. I am at peace."

Patrick's business belly flop was similar to Harold's, but their stories go two very different directions.

"I was one of those bright, young entrepreneurs you read about in *Forbes* or *Fortune* magazine," Patrick explained. "I grew bored with and tired of my upper-management job in corporate America, so I walked away and started my own business from scratch. It was a brilliant idea—providing a specialized service to Realtors. With the real-estate boom in the late eighties, we were making money as fast as we could shovel it in."

He paused, looked down at his hands, and continued. "No one planned on the real-estate market drying up like it did here in southern California. Suddenly all that money was nowhere to be found. We were struggling to make payroll each month. Eventually we laid off 80 percent of our workforce. We kept hoping and praying the economy would turn around quickly.

"It didn't. We had to declare bankruptcy and shut down. It was the darkest period of my life. I told my wife I needed some time alone, and I took off to a friend's cabin in northern Michigan. I sat all alone in that drafty old cabin for three weeks. I didn't shave, rarely bathed or ate, just sat around in total desperation.

"When I finally returned to L.A. I started making the rounds of all my old cronies in the corporate scene. I soon discovered I was one of thousands of white-collar workers out of work. This compounded my dilemma, for I was overqualified for just about every job out there.

"It was so difficult to be unemployed. I frequently contemplated suicide—it was that humiliating. As time wore on, I found the need to adjust my expectations. It was clear I wasn't going to land an upper-management job like the one I desired. So I got a little distance from the whole thing and made a decision.

"I started applying for middle-management positions. I would delete certain parts of my résumé so I didn't look overqualified. Before long I landed a position with my old employer's biggest competitor. It's kind of ironic . . . working for the competition. But the big adjustment for me was the demotion to middle management. I'm making about half of what I made before and working every bit as hard. It was hard at first, but as time has passed, I've accepted my new position and I can even say I'm at peace about it. At least I can say I'm working and that's a lot to be grateful for."

When Gigi walked into her doctor's office for her annual mammogram, she had no indication this visit would be any different from any other over the last twelve years. But her whole world was to change in a most serious way.

"There's a lump that will require a biopsy," the doctor informed her. "There's no need to worry because we won't know anything until we get the results back. I'll call you the moment the tests come back."

When the nurse called Gigi and told her to come to the office, she knew that was a bad omen. "It's malignant," the doctor said. "We'll need to operate. I recommend we do that as quickly as possible."

Gigi was so upset, it was as if she were in shock. Going through her daily routine, she could barely recall what she had done fifteen minutes before. She prepared for the surgery as best she could.

"I remember my husband and kids all kissing me before I went into the operating room. They all told me that everything was going to be okay," Gigi recalled, wiping her eyes.

"When I regained consciousness after the operation, my doctor was there to tell me more news. I just wanted to hear that they got it all. He said just the opposite. He told me cancer was running rampant all over my body. I was sick, physically, mentally, and emotionally. It was utter devastation.

"It was such an amazing time for me. I knew I had

to grieve the loss of my body and ultimately my life. God was gracious to me in enabling me to work through those feelings in a relatively short time. I realized that time was going to be my most precious commodity, so I cherished it.

"The longer I lived with my cancer, the more I was able to accept it. I became thankful for each and every day I awoke. I made time for the precious moments I wanted to remember with my husband and sweet little ones. It wasn't long before I came to accept the fact that it would do me no good to be angry, bitter, or vengeful.

"I made peace with my situation on a sunny summer afternoon in August," she recalls. "I said, 'Lord, I want to live each day to the fullest. Help me to put aside anything that will keep me from doing that.'"

"God answered my prayer. These last few months have been the most wonderful gift any woman or man could ever receive. I am a fortunate person."

Those were some of Gigi's last words. Her husband, Kelly, shared them at her funeral service. She inspired many with her positive outlook, even though life didn't turn out the way she planned.

Time and distance provide perspective. For some, time will bring a happy ending, for others it will be a peaceful ending. Either way, for most of us the ending is beyond our control. It's all in God's hands.

TIME AND STILLNESS

As a child, I grew up learning many of the rich verses in the Scriptures. Back then, in my neck of the woods there was only one Bible to read—the old King James Version. One of my favorites was tucked away in the forty-sixth Psalm: "Be still, and know that I am God."[1]

I've always liked that verse, but after enduring my crisis, I've come to love it. I tend to be a "churner," and the stillness that can only come from God is something I am learning about more and more each day.

It's interesting to me that ever since my seminary days, I've gravitated to the New American Standard version of the Scriptures, and that verse reads a little differently in that translation: "Cease striving and know that I am God."

The Lord must have known that I needed a crisis in my life to bring me to the place where my striving would rise off the top of the chart. And it was through that rising that I saw my overwhelming need for stillness. So after the crisis came the time and distance necessary to bring me to the place of peace and stillness that I live in today.

As I pen these words today, I am on the top of Camelback Mountain, knowing full well that even on the peak, I am always remarkably close to another journey that could begin at the lowest point.

The difference? Time and distance.

CHAPTer 4

Focus on What You Have, Not on What You DON'T HAVE

Security is mostly a superstition. It does not exist in nature, nor do the children of men as a whole experience it. Avoiding danger is no safer in the long run than outright exposure. Life is either a daring adventure . . . or nothing.

—*Helen Keller*

For someone who has faced life's disappointments, there will always be reminders of the pain. A treasured picture of someone you lost. A certain song that plays on the radio. A fragrance in the air. A child's toy or a deed to a house. It may be a particular day of the year, a birthday, an anniversary, or a holiday that was of special significance before the crisis hit.

Personally, I've got a ton of memories that I'm still reprogramming into the new files of my life. But certain feelings die slowly, and I guess that's just natural when you go through a difficult time.

February fourteenth was always a fun day for me. For the last twenty years I particularly enjoyed the challenge of making each Valentine's Day a little different—and a little better than the last one. It was a tailor-made occasion for lovers, and I relished it.

I have now discovered that February fourteenth is not that much fun for a person who is single, unattached, uninvolved, and basically on his own. I am fortunate to have kids—we pass Valentines back and forth. But anyone who identifies with this circumstance realizes it's not quite the occasion it once was.

I remember one of the first Valentine's Days I experienced as a newly single person. A friend had hired me to do some consulting work with him, so I agreed to fly to the Midwest to meet with him and some others for a planning session. February fourteenth would fall right smack in the middle of this three-day meeting, so I had hopes that I could fulfill a workaholic's fantasy: Work Valentine's Day away without giving it a second thought.

I arrived the night of the thirteenth and was taken to a beautiful mountain resort, where we would be meeting for our sessions. As the sun came up on the fourteenth, I walked out of my room and the view took my breath away. I thanked God for allowing me to be in such a glorious setting.

Our all-day think tank was extremely productive. By seven o'clock that evening, we had accomplished more than we expected to in the entire three-day time frame. My friend glanced at his watch and suddenly blurted out, "Oh no, look at the time! I told my wife I'd take her out for dinner since it's Valentine's Day. You guys will have to excuse me, I gotta run or I'll be in big trouble!"

Several other guys at our meeting begged off with the same story. In a matter of three minutes, the entire circle of men had cleared out, leaving me and one other out-of-town guest, a guy named Randy.

We stared at each other quietly for a minute. Then Randy broke the silence with a suggestion: "I hear they have a great restaurant here at the resort. Let me take a minute or two to call my wife back home, then whattya say you and me go downstairs and throw ourselves a little party?"

I liked the way this guy was thinking. Both of us were a little sad, sitting in a hotel room in a distant state, with no hopes of any Valentine's frivolity. He was sad because he had to be away from his wife, and I was sad because I had no wife to be away from. We were one exciting duo.

He made his phone call, we washed up, retied our ties (we heard this was a fancy place—"Gentlemen, coats and ties, please!"), and made our way downstairs. After a two-minute walk, we arrived at the lobby in front of the restaurant. Randy walked right up to the maître d' and asked for a table for two. "But of course, sir.

Tonight we have nothing but tables for two." He then led us to our table, located in just about the best spot in the whole restaurant—right by a majestic old fireplace, with an inviting fire crackling away.

Randy followed the maître d' to the table and I joined the procession right behind him. It was my addition to this parade that was creating quite a stir throughout the restaurant. I quickly checked to see if my shirttail was hanging out or my zipper was down or I had my suit coat on inside out, but everything checked out A-OK.

It wasn't until we were both seated at the table that it hit us—at the same time—*we were the only table in the entire restaurant that wasn't a Valentine's Day couple!*

The moment we understood, we hung our heads in embarrassment. Husbands and wives, boyfriends and girlfriends were craning their necks to see if they recognized this male couple that strolled into a Valentine's Day celebration.

The restaurant staff was in a real dither. A hostess was making her way to each table, presenting each lovely lady with a red rose, compliments of the management. Almost as soon as we sat down, her path brought her to our table. She halted nervously, cleared her throat, and asked, "Which one of you would like a red rose?"

I thought I was more embarrassed than Randy, but he proved me wrong by speaking loud enough for everyone to hear, "Not me—we're here from out of town. I'm from Texas . . . he's from California!"

He pointed to me as he said the word *California*. Just the mention of that word triggered a knee-jerk reaction by all the couples in this quaint Midwest locale. They turned to talk quietly to each other. I could hear whispers, but the only word I could make out was the word *California*, as if that in itself provided the necessary explanation for the entire situation.

By now Randy and I were sweating like pigs. "Gee, it's kinda warm here by the fire," I said, lamely attempting casual conversation. It wasn't working. We were out of place. We both mopped buckets of perspiration off our foreheads with our pink linen napkins.

Now the waiter worked up enough courage to approach us. "Tell me about your specials this evening," I said. I wanted to take the attention away from the two-male dilemma and focus on the main reason we were there in the first place: food. It was the wrong question to ask. "Tonight all of our specials are dinners for two. We will start you off with champagne and then proceed to toss an elegant Caesar salad for two right at your table. We will then bring any entrée of your choice in double portion followed by one of our famous flaming desserts."

"I'll take the biggest steak you've got," Randy interrupted. He had heard all he cared to of "dinners for two." I also noticed that he once again said everything loud enough for all the diners to hear. Apparently, he felt it was an appropriate strategy to reestablish himself as a Texan who lived off meat and potatoes.

"I'll take the same thing," I said when it was my turn. Randy looked disappointed that I would order the same thing (what will people think?), so I hastily changed my order to prime rib.

"King's cut, or queen's, sir?" our waiter asked.

"King's cut. Definitely."

When the waiter left our table, we both laughed nervously at what was transpiring before our very eyes. "My wife's never gonna believe this!" Randy confessed, twisting his cloth napkin into the tightest knot he could. It looked like he was wringing out a mop as a steady trickle of liquid flowed from the linen.

"Yeah, this is definitely strange, all right," I replied.

We continued our vain attempts at conversation. Randy became more comfortable as the dinner progressed, but I was as stiff as a ramrod the whole evening. Looking back now, I feel sorry about the company I must have been that evening. I certainly did nothing to make it any easier on Randy.

Two men have never put away food quicker than the two of us did. I complimented Randy on the suggestion to our waiter that he bring the check when he brought the entrée. We scarfed and were out of there in record time. As we walked out Randy made one final loud statement, "I'm going back to my hotel room. And you're going back to your hotel room, right? Okay, see you tomorrow at our business meeting!"

I went back to my room, threw off my coat with disgust, took off my tie with enough anger to choke myself. Like a silly little kid, I plopped on the hotel bed, buried my head in the pillow, and began to cry like a baby. The only sounds that could be heard were from my weeping, but inside my mind I was screaming at the top of my lungs: *Why do I have to be the one person in the whole stinking restaurant to be without a Valentine? Why did it have to be* my *marriage that failed?*

THE PERIL OF THE PITY PARTY

Whenever you go through a disappointment in life, it is very natural to feel sorry for yourself. My incident at that Valentine's dinner was just the tip of the iceberg for me. I spent quite a bit of time overcome with self-pity.

As I look back on that particular period of time in my life, I have begun to realize that there is a fine line—a tightrope—that we walk when we go through those types of strong feelings and emotions.

On one hand, people do need the freedom to work through their losses and feel their pain. As I said in the last chapter, this is known as the grieving process.

But if we re not careful, this process can sidetrack

80

us into a full-blown pity party, complete with all the sadness and depression that accompanies it.

"When the doctors told me I would have to live with diabetes, I went into an emotional tailspin," Herb recalled. "Looking back now, it all seems a little foolish. Being told that you have a condition that can be controlled by regular medication is so much better than getting the news that you have a terminal illness."

"My pity party aged me," Herb confessed. "I was fifty-six when I was given the news. My wife says I went from fifty-six to eighty-six in one afternoon. I guess she was right. It completely took the wind out of my sail."

Herb's wife, Shirley, knew him well enough to read between the lines. "This was all about *aging* to Herb," she observes. "The real issue wasn't diabetes, it was a man in his mid-fifties who had to accept the fact that he was growing older—not even growing old, but *older*. He resisted every step of the way. When he turned thirty-five, he was unusually quiet and upset. Forty was worse. Fifty was a nightmare.

"He seemed to get a handle on it the last few years," she continued. "It was like he thought he beat the system, because he was still in perfect health.

"When he was told of his diabetes, it was like slapping a giant black mark across his record. He started to wallow in a pool of self-pity to the point I thought he was going to drown in it. I knew he was in trouble the day he said to me, 'Shirley, I might as well have inoperable, terminal cancer. . . . I'm just gonna die anyway.'"

Herb had fallen off his tightrope. He was beyond grieving the loss of his youth. He was neck-deep in pity's mud.

HEALTHY WAYS TO COPE
WITH THE GRIEF

The experts are pretty united on this subject: Holidays are especially difficult for a person going through the grieving process. Therefore, before we move on with our cautions against self-pity, let's look at some positive, practical ways for folks to deal with holiday grief, which can be all-consuming.

First, your physical health is paramount. It is vital that you get your required amount of rest. Some folks oversleep, and that isn't healthy either, but many others attempt to deny their pain by jumping headfirst into their jobs. Consequently, they overwork, minimize sleep, and eventually face complete exhaustion. Watch out. When you get physically down, pretty soon you'll get emotionally down.

Second, your diet is important. Eating healthy meals at regular times is something you may tend to toss out the window, but there is danger in doing so. I recall how sorry I felt for myself, and one of the ways I acted it out was by not cooking. *I'll just eat fast food or a microwaved something or other,* I remember rationalizing.

Hidden beneath that was the message, *I'm not good enough to cook for,* and *I don't deserve a nice, healthy meal.* Shame on me. That'll hurt in the long run. Then, more than ever, I needed the benefits of a well-balanced diet.

Exercise is another way to keep you going. This is a constant struggle for me, since I don't exercise a lot when I'm feeling *good.* The trick is finding the activity that works best for you, be it a stationary bike, a morning jog, an afternoon tennis game, an evening stroll, or an aerobic workout at a nearby health club. Try to remain as consistent as possible.

I fell into an awkward situation at the restaurant on Valentine's Day, but in many ways it was good that I got out of my room to mingle with folks. A danger when you're in this frame of mind is isolating yourself—so don't. Schedule activities with your favorite people so the time around the holidays won't feel so long and drawn out. Part of my discovery was how many folks *don't* have plans on particular holidays and how they would love to do something fun in order to pass the time. Sure, there's a little risk involved. You have to put yourself out there a bit. But it often pays rich dividends.

Some experts have even suggested that you choose a time before the holiday to allow all the memories and feelings to come to the forefront. The idea is to deal with the feelings rather than stuffing them back down inside, pretending they are not really there. This is easier said than done, so be careful with this one; try to have someone around to help you.

I worked so hard at establishing traditions within our home that the thought of altering them seemed sacrilegious. Obviously, we've had to change some of the ways we celebrate Thanksgiving and Christmas and birthdays. Change isn't bad. I always thought it was, but I'm learning that is not the case. It goes back to flexing and learning to go with the flow.

One final thought on this subject: Grieving will usually take longer than anyone thinks it will. Go easy on yourself in this regard. Saying things like, "I should be over all this by now" and "It's time to get on with my life" is helpful, but processing grief takes a lot of energy, and that may make it difficult for you to function in the way you are used to. Work hard at *accepting* what has taken place. Look for God in all of it.

BEING THANKFUL FOR WHAT YOU HAVE

Part of what takes grief into pity is crossing the line into dwelling on what I *don't* have. The scenarios are many and varied, but they all carry the identical theme: "If I could have received that promotion, it would've meant a handsome increase in my salary. We had a hundred different ways we were going to spend that extra money. We were going to remodel the kitchen, do some landscaping, build a redwood deck off the back of the house, and finally take a real vacation. None of that will happen now, since they passed me over for the promotion. . . ."

"We were going to be the perfect family. We were going to raise fabulous kids and have a marriage that everyone wished was theirs. It's hard to be the model family when my husband can't control his alcohol intake. Dreams of being envied as the family living in the cute house surrounded by the white picket-fence were replaced by the reality of being pitied as I helped a staggering alcoholic into the house after he made a scene in the front yard—just inside the white picket-fence. . . ."

"I had all these glorious notions of what it would be like when we were grandparents. I never dreamed my kids would move so far away from me. Seeing the grandkids was supposed to be a daily occurrence. Now it's turned into a once-a-year quick trip. Nobody else sees their grandkids so little."

My friend Stephen is a forty-four-year-old professional in the Seattle area. He was born and raised there, and with the exception of attending college back East, he has always lived there. He married Kendra when they were both in their mid-twenties. They have three adorable children, who actually do some modeling for children's clothing catalogs. They live in an upscale suburb where the kids attend a fairly exclusive private

school. Stephen has always been an extremely successful businessman, driving the right kind of car, wearing
designer clothes, swinging the top brand of golf clubs,
eating at the trendiest of restaurants, and always the
first in his neighborhood with the newest of toys.

"That's why the bankruptcy of my business was so
devastating," Stephen admitted. He shrugged his
shoulders and held up his right index finger as he said,
"It was the *very first time* I had ever failed at anything.
Can you imagine? Forty-four years of having things
pretty much go my own way!"

He looked down at his Ralph Lauren shirt and
Italian loafers and shook his head. "I know lots of other
guys who have lost their businesses. Shoot, I know guys
who have lost five and six businesses in as many years.
But it was so very different for me because I had never
lost anything before. I didn't know how to fail.

"Consequently I created a major pool of self-pity.
I saw all these other guys and gals around me in the
exact same situation—total financial devastation—but
I rationalized myself deeper and deeper into the muck
by saying, '*None* of those other folks has had to deal
with the same emotions I'm dealing with. They know
what it means to lose. I'm not saying they are losers,
but I am definitely a winner. And winners don't go
broke. I just can't deal with this mess.'"

But dealing with it is exactly what Stephen had to
do. Once he got to the point that he could pull himself

out of the muddy, murky pity pit, he was able to take stock of his life.

"I was raised in a small Baptist church. As a kid I always used to sing the old hymn, 'Count Your Blessings.' Part of the chorus goes, 'Count your blessings, name them one by one, and it will surprise you what the Lord has done.'[1]

"I began to do just that. I started thinking about all that I had to be grateful for. Now I realize that is a standard recommendation when you're going through loss, but it was brand-new stuff for me. Focusing on what I had was the major method I used to get through the catastrophe."

I experienced the same sorts of emotions. I didn't want my marriage to end and I felt robbed when it did. I went into a fairly major pity party and in doing so I wasn't very fair to anyone at the time, and I was a pretty miserable guy on top of it.

I happened to overhear two of my kids talking one day and their words stung. "Dad's not much fun to be around these days," was all they said, but it was enough. If I wasn't careful, self-pity was going to drive away the five most important people in my life.

Slowly, but steadily, I started reassessing my life. In particular, I began focusing on what I still had that made my life special.

I had my health. If I watched what I ate and remembered to exercise, I generally felt pretty good.

(Plus, if I was ever going to meet someone new for my life, I didn't want to look like the Goodyear Blimp!)

I had my kids. Every one of them was dealing with this situation in his or her own distinct way, but not one of them pulled back from expressing love for me. I saw unconditional acceptance in one of its purest forms as I watched these four crazy guys and that one gorgeous girl love me back to life.

I had friends. This was to be such an overwhelming blessing to me that I have chosen to devote an entire chapter to it. At this point, suffice it to say that God put some men and women in my life to bring me back from the brink of pity and despair.

I had God. I know many people drift away from the Lord during difficult times, but I also know that many others feel drawn closer to Him. The latter was the case for me and it was wonderful to feel God feed my soul in ways I had never before experienced. It was a spiritual renewal for me, now that I look back on it.

When I began to concentrate on what I had as opposed to what I didn't, I was able to gain perspective and objectivity. And it was also at that time that circumstances seemed to improve so that I truly could get on with my life.

I also began to realize the sobering fact that there were lots of people who had it worse than I did. Part of the self-pity came from daily convincing myself that no one in the world was being asked to endure more crippling circumstances than I was.

Pity had created blinders on my eyes. When I removed them, I saw many people who were being put through the sort of pain that made my hurt look like a little kid's boo-boo. Not only was I mistaken to be in such self-pity, I actually needed to thank God for blessing me the way He was. It was time to wake up and smell the coffee.

A MEMORABLE NIGHT AT THE MOVIES

One of the blessings of my new life was that I certainly didn't have a lot of free time to sit around with nothing to do. With five active children, four of them teenagers, life was far from dull. Each morning I woke up, stumbled to the kitchen in my robe and curlers, packed five lunches, woke everyone up at their appointed times, made sure everyone had their schoolwork for the day, signed any number of school forms, and quickly caught everyone's schedule so we could have an evening meal together. Between basketball, jazz choir, church activities, homework, soccer, football, and a host of other activities, each day contained enough excitement to ensure that I would absolutely collapse into bed each night!

We all worked hard at having dinner together most evenings. It's the only time there is even the slightest chance of having the six of us in one room for more than three minutes. That's why it was so unusual when all six of us were together for something other than a meal.

But it was one of those occasions that marked us in a special way. One of the kids had the TV remote control (the ultimate sign of power in our place) and was casually surfing the channels at eight o'clock one evening. For some reason, he stopped as a network made-for-TV movie was being introduced.

I was about to ask him to keep going when I stopped abruptly. Rather than the typical made-for-TV movie fare, this wasn't about the murder or disease of the week. It was *The Dennis Byrd Story*, the movie chronicling the tragic neck injury suffered by one of the brightest lights in the New York Jets lineup. Without my intervening, the child with the remote stopped his surfing right there and we began to watch the show unfold. What was particularly intriguing to me was that the entire family seemed unusually interested in this story and all six of us ended up on the couch before the end of the opening credits.

We were quickly mesmerized by this teleplay. Such a likable guy, a country boy in the big city, it didn't take long for a viewer to become a Dennis Byrd fan. A kid with solid Midwestern values and a Christian upbringing, he married his high-school sweetheart and went to the Jets in the NFL draft.

Naturally, the main drama in the movie centered

around his neck injury. It was so severe, it left him paralyzed from the neck down. But the greatest test of his faith did not deter Dennis Byrd. The movie concluded with his victorious walk into a press conference, proving to all the world that he could beat the odds. It was the kind of movie that made you want to stand up and cheer.

All six of us were openly weeping at several different junctures of the show. That's not a normal occurrence at our house.

"That poor man," one of the kids whispered.

"Will he ever get out of that wheelchair?" asked another.

"This is sad," is all one of my boys could say.

When it was over, even with the triumphant ending, we all sat in a stunned silence.

I can't speak for the five kids, but I think I have a pretty good hunch what it was that they were thinking: No matter how hard their lives may be at this particular time, after seeing what that dear family endured, there was no way we could sit on that couch and feel sorry for ourselves. Sure, all of us had been through some pretty traumatic stuff over the last few months, but look how much worse it could have been! Six people got their wake-up call that evening.

I'm sure glad the six of us saw that movie together.

There was a lesson in it for all of us . . . especially Dad.

CHAPTer 5

Life
Will Often Be
out of Your
CONTROL

When through fiery trials thy pathway shall lie
My grace all-sufficient shall be thy supply.
The flame shall not hurt thee, I only design
Thy dross to consume and thy gold to refine.

—*George Keith*

I didn't fully realize the scope of emotion I saw in the eyes of my father and mother the day I turned sixteen . . . until the day one of my children turned sixteen. That year is the magical number for children of the United States of America for one overwhelming reason.

They are now old enough to drive.

I can still recall learning how to drive from my father. As he patiently sat in the passenger seat of our 1965 Ford Falcon, every muscle in his face was tight as a drum and an inordinate amount of perspiration was blanketing his brow, especially on a winter's afternoon in Philadelphia.

Certain parts of the driving experience went well for me. I pushed the accelerator and the brake pedal well. I mastered readjusting the rearview mirror like a seasoned veteran. From there it got iffy. I did not shift gears very well (we would eventually change to automatic transmission as a self-esteem issue) and still worse, parallel parking was like a scene from a horror movie.

One nervous kid showed up at the Pennsylvania State Police station to take his driver's test that following summer. My mouth was parched and my shirt was soaked as I led the officer to the car for my test.

I remember the officer getting in on the passenger side, removing his hat, khaki in color—just like the rest of his uniform—one of those large brimmed, Smokey-the-Bear models, and placing the hat on the front seat between us. That hat was a silent reminder of the power vested him by the state of Pennsylvania. With that hat staring up at me from its place on the seat, I realized he could flunk me just because he didn't like fat kids with blond hair.

"Let me see your learner's permit, son," the officer stated in matter-of-fact tones, never changing expression.

"Yes, sir," I replied, my voice cracking in a way it hadn't since I was a thirteen-year-old geek.

He immediately frowned and I began to stress even more. "What is your first name, son?"

"William."

"Can you tell me why your first name is only listed as an initial?" His brow was furrowed into washboard ripples above his beady brown eyes.

"I think it might be because my last name is so long—and because I am a 'junior,' and we wanted to make a distinction between my dad and me." I honestly hadn't given my permit a lot of thought.

"So I see," he mused. "W. J. Butterworth, Jr. Is it important to you that 'Jr.' be stated on there?"

"Yes, sir," I replied and then attempted a little humor. "If my dad gets a ticket, I don't want it to appear on my record." (As if my dad, the world's safest driver, would ever get a ticket for any possible infraction of the law. My dad was the most law-abiding guy I knew.)

"Well, I believe it is possible to get 'William' and 'Jr.' on the first line of your learner's permit."

I waited in silence.

"Do you also need your middle initial?"

"Yes, sir, if it's not too much trouble."

"Let me figure this out a little." He became totally consumed by the small, permit-sized card now resting on his clipboard. Then he added, "You can go ahead and begin driving, son. Just follow the white lines."

As I nervously began my journey, I couldn't help but observe that something was happening in my favor

... the officer was absolutely transfixed by my permit. All of life was going by and he was completely oblivious to it.

This became more apparent as I started revealing my little nervous driving habits. Things like knocking down the fluorescent-orange plastic cones that are supposed to remain upright. Other things like forgetting to engage my directional signal when making a turn. Even driving a couple of my wheels up onto the curb while attempting the difficult maneuver known as the parallel park.

The entire time I glanced out of the corner of my eye, wondering how this was going over with my personal policeman. I could hear the officer counting out the letters in my name. "W, I, L, L, I, A, M, space; J, period, space; B, U, T, T, E, R, W, O, R, T, H, space; J, R, period."

In a few minutes the test was over. The officer had not given a second thought to my driving ability. Despite my making the full spectrum of driving mistakes, he jumped out of the car, saying, "Well, you're right, son, your first name doesn't fit on the first line of your permit. So we'll just have to keep it the way it is for your driver's license."

And then he uttered the magic words every sixteen-year-old dreams of: "Congratulations, son . . . you pass!"

It was another one of those "go with the flow" moments. I was overjoyed that a driver like myself could be so uniquely unqualified yet legally allowed access to all the world's roads.

So I guess that's why my parents looked the way they did the first night I drove off with their car. When my daughter, Joy, turned sixteen, I remember seeing her drive off and feeling similar feelings (and unlike me, she was a *good* driver!).

The feeling? *Lack of control.* At that benchmark age of sixteen, children visually illustrate to their parents that they are no longer exclusively under our control. They have taken some of life by the throat and intend to go with it.

THE LINGERING LESSON

Probably one of the most difficult lessons for me to learn in my catastrophe was that so much of what happened was completely out of my control. A lot of us like to be in control; thus when something comes into our lives that is beyond our grasp, it can absolutely destroy us. This was my case.

I never felt that I was a dominating, all-powerful, controlling type person, but then again, I wasn't married to me for all those years. I'm still not clear on all that from the past, but I do know that as my marriage was unraveling, I panicked and began to react strongly to my wife's need for increased distance by trying to cling even tighter than I had previously.

I was bowled over by the loss of control in this

situation. The counselor I was seeing really began to grill me on this point. He began saying, "Bill, remember, in any relationship it takes two to say 'yes,' but only one to say 'no.'"

Then he would pause for effect and continue, "It sounds like Rhonda is saying 'no,' and you are unwilling to accept it."

"But I don't want my marriage to end," I protested. My eyes would glaze over and my lip would start to tremble.

"I know that," he replied softly, "and I think Rhonda knows that as well. But she is saying 'no' and you seem to be responding by shouting 'yes' even louder than you've ever shouted it before."

"I guess that's a fair assessment."

"The truth is, Bill," he continued, "no matter how long and loud you scream 'yes,' it's not going to change her 'no.' This decision is completely out of your hands. Try as you might, you cannot control her."

I was both sad and embarrassed—sad that I couldn't control her and embarrassed that I wanted to. It sounded so devious.

WHO'S REALLY IN CONTROL HERE?

Human beings have struggled with the control issue from day one. Adam and Eve got into the original predicament. In their pride they thought, *We don't need God, we can take care of everything all by ourselves, thank you!*

And from there it's been an uphill battle to learn to let go and give the ultimate control of life to the Person it rightfully belongs to.

In the Old Testament days following the split in the kingdom of Israel, God raised up men called prophets to speak to the people, confronting them about their unwillingness to trust Him. The Israelites wanted control of their lives and their stubbornness had already divided the kingdom into Israel up north and Judah to the south.

Jeremiah was one of those prophets. He was chosen by God from his home in the southern kingdom of Judah to make both Israel and Judah aware of their sinfulness. In many occasions in Jeremiah's book, God had Jeremiah actually *experience* the lesson He wanted him to learn. One of the better-known visual aids God used with Jeremiah is found in the eighteenth chapter:

> The word which came to Jeremiah from the LORD, saying, "Arise and go down to the potter's house, and there I shall announce My words to you." Then I went down to the potter's house, and there he was, making something on the wheel. But the vessel that he was making of clay was spoiled in the hand of the potter; so he remade it into another vessel, as it pleased the potter to make.
>
> Then the word of the LORD came to me saying, "Can I not, O house of Israel, deal with you as this potter

does?" declares the LORD. "Behold, like the clay in the potter's hand, so are you in My hand, O house of Israel. At one moment I might speak concerning a nation or concerning a kingdom to uproot, to pull down, or to destroy it; if that nation against which I have spoken turns from its evil, I will relent concerning the calamity I planned to bring on it. Or at another moment I might speak concerning a nation or concerning a kingdom to build up or to plant it; if it does evil in My sight by not obeying My voice, then I will think better of the good with which I had promised to bless it." [1]

Most of us don't traffic much in the pottery scene. An occasional visit to a craft fair at the local mall might bring us in contact with a potter on display between a woodcutter and a needlepointer. Or we may have seen a Native American display his or her mastery of the wheel at a local reservation. But beyond that the whole concept of making pots from clay is not one that is very contemporary.

But it was extremely contemporary to the people of Jeremiah's day. A potter's wheel was as meaningful to them as a laptop, modem, and laser printer are to us. And through this lesson from the potter, God was able to teach Jeremiah a truth he would not forget, thus ensuring he would make an even greater impact on his audience. Any trained educator worth his or her salt will tell you, personally experiencing a lesson raises the level of a follow-up speech quite a few notches.

The timing was not accidental. When Jeremiah arrived at the potter's, the craftsman was at a place with a vessel where it was "spoiled." If you've ever seen what happens next, you'll know that I choose the word carefully. . . .

The potter *squashes* the vessel of clay back into a big ol' wet lump, turning round and round on the wheel.

But soon, that lump is taking on a new and better shape than it did before it was so forcefully crushed.

I think the lingering lesson of this passage is the need for a clay vessel to be *moldable*. Control freaks have serious tendencies toward rigidity. I am learning that I cannot control everything that happens in my life. Only God can do that. Granted, there are some things I can do to *influence* what happens, but that is something very different.

God is the One who is in charge. He leads us along, step by step. I find that I need to read statements like that over and over again. *I'm* not in charge, He is. *I'm* not leading Him, He's leading me.

My role is to be moldable, teachable, ready to take the shape that He forms with His hands. Anything more than that pliability is overstepping my bounds, and if I'm not careful, He'll have to step in with more drastic lessons.

Life's Fragile Nature

I just heard on the news this morning of a national leader who was being recognized for her years of service to the United States. She stood on the platform, being lauded by a line of fellow workers and political partners. The climax of the program was to be the presentation of a beautiful, one-of-a-kind, hand-crafted Waterford crystal statue of an American bald eagle with wings spread in flight. As the presenter made his way to the dais, he brushed too closely to the award and a room full of people watched in horror as the eagle fell to the floor, shattering into thousands of minuscule pieces!

Since many of us don't see ourselves as Waterford crystal, perhaps an old clay pot would be more appropriate. God's lesson to Jeremiah was not finished in chapter eighteen. Chapter nineteen records another adventure with "earthenware" (clay pots) that Jeremiah observed firsthand:

> Thus says the LORD: "Go and buy a potter's earthenware jar, and take some of the elders of the people and some of the senior priests. Then go out to the valley of Ben-hinnom, which is by the entrance of the potsherd gate; and proclaim there the words that I shall tell you, and say, 'Hear the word of the LORD, O kings of Judah and inhabitants of Jerusalem: thus says the LORD of hosts, the God of Israel, "Behold I am about to bring a calamity upon this place, at which the ears of everyone that hears of it will tingle.

Because they have forsaken Me and have made this an alien place and have burned sacrifices in it to other gods that neither they nor their forefathers nor the kings of Judah had ever known, and because they have filled this place with the blood of the innocent . . .

"I shall also make this city a desolation and an object of hissing; everyone who passes by it will be astonished and hiss because of all its disasters. . . .

"Then you are to break the jar in the sight of the men who accompany you and say to them, 'Thus says the LORD of hosts, " Just so shall I break this people and this city, even as one breaks a potter's vessel, which cannot again be repaired; and they will bury in Topheth because there is no other place for burial'"." [2]

Yikes! It's the Old Testament version of the shattered crystal eagle! And God was the One who did the pushing. Can't you just envision old Jeremiah taking that clay jar and dramatically smashing it on the ground! Talk about an attention getter . . . that one would turn some heads.

I think there is another important lesson to be understood here. Not only did God want Jeremiah to know that clay was to be moldable, He also wanted him to know that clay was *breakable*.

For many of us who have endured the crises, the

catastrophes, the disappointments of life, we know that feeling. We have been broken.

For some, the breaking has felt like a complete crushing of life. Nevertheless, after some time has passed, there has been the hope of a rebirth, a second chance, a phoenix rising from the ashes. And in all these cases, there is the unmistakable hand of God, guiding the clay to its higher purpose.

Records tell us that when the Roman catacombs were first discovered, the historians came upon a variety of crudely painted pictures on the inner walls of the caves where early Christians had been imprisoned before their cruel tortures for embracing their faith. The most famous figure discovered was the "fish" symbol with the inscription "Ichthus" within it. To this day, these primitive drawings grace churches, homes, wallets, key chains, and the ubiquitous bumper stickers.

Second only to the fish was another crudely painted sketch: a man with an animal nestled around his neck, resting on his shoulders. The image symbolized the shepherd and a sheep, another familiar metaphor of our relationship with Christ. What is especially intriguing about this image is the common thinking of the day concerning shepherds. At that time, there was only one occasion for a shepherd to have a sheep on his shoulders. If a sheep was not following his shepherd and instead going his own way, the shepherd would very graphically demonstrate to the sheep the danger in not following him. History records that a shepherd would take a wandering sheep and literally break one of its legs, so that it would no longer stray from the appointed path. Of course, a sheep couldn't maneuver very well with a broken leg, so the shepherd would pick it up and carry it for the time period necessary for healing to take place.

The applications from this sort of story are myriad. The broken leg, and the broken pot, were both instigated by God over this very issue of *control*. "Who's in charge here?" is a fair question for the pot, the potter, the sheep, and the shepherd.

Especially in the shepherd/sheep scenario, the breaking led to an even more intimate relationship between the two of them. This was exactly the case in my situation. I found that my crisis drove me even closer to my Father than ever before. It is also completely appropriate to say that the crisis was *necessary* for us to arrive at that closeness.

Brokenness is a state to which no one aspires. It is usually brought on us without invitation, and we feel like a jar plummeting to the ground and dashed into pieces. It hurts, it's extremely unflattering, and it immediately conjures up the question, "Why?"

God doesn't always answer that question; He has never guaranteed anywhere in Scripture that He must do so. But for many of us the question's answer could very well center around our need to let go of the reins and in doing so, relinquish control.

A century before Jeremiah wrote his words, the prophet Isaiah offered another insight on the smashing of a clay pot:

"Therefore this iniquity will be to you
Like a breach about to fall,
A bulge in a high wall,
Whose collapse comes suddenly in an instant.
And whose collapse is like the smashing of a potter's jar; So ruthlessly shattered
That a sherd will not be found among its pieces
To take fire from a hearth,
Or to scoop water from a cistern."

For thus the Lord GOD, the Holy One of Israel, has said,
"In repentance and rest you shall be saved,
In quietness and trust is your strength."
But you were not willing . . .[3]

We take smashing to a new level here. There are two types of smashing being discussed by Isaiah. He is specifically referring to a smash so brutal—"ruthlessly shattered"—the pottery has no more use. But he refers to the opposite in the phrases, "take fire from a hearth" and "scoop water from a cistern." Here he talks about a shattered piece of pottery that no longer functions as it used to but instead *it has a new usefulness*.

Don't miss this, for it is significant. This passage suggests that many of us have endured the smashing experience without being completely crushed, but rather, redefined. What was once a lovely jar, handsomely displayed, beautifully designed, was suddenly redirected in life after a crash of monumental proportions. But rather than being completely discarded, a piece remained, a *sherd*, as it is called in the text. And that piece can perform different tasks than could the whole jar. Perhaps it is taking ashes from a hearth or scooping water from a well. The point is, that piece of pottery still has a purpose, maybe not as glorious, but of equal value and importance in the home. It survived the "ruthless shattering" for a reason.

I came from a jar lifestyle. But God saw that I had too many tendencies toward control as a jar and so He, in His wisdom, has chosen to use my breaking as an opportunity to correct some of those tendencies as well as keep me useful. Now I am more like a shovel. And I am learning that it is easier to surrender to Him in issues of control when I am a scooper, in contrast to my life when I was a jar.

No one plans for catastrophe, yet many of us who have been through it now see we would be lesser people without it.

Go figure.

STORMS OF PERFECTION

When a good friend of mine heard about the direction I was taking in writing this book, he said, "Bill, I've got to send you a copy of a book called *Storms of Perfection* by Andy Andrews."[4] I had not heard of the book, but once I received a copy of it, I immediately understood why my friend sent it.

The book is a collection of letters from over fifty people representing a variety of professions: actors, singers, sports stars, business folk, ministers, writers, entrepreneurs, and politicians. Every one of these people would be considered a success in his or her field of endeavor. Andy wrote them a letter asking them to tell him their biggest problem or greatest rejection. What he received from these people were dozens of their personal stories not only describing their biggest problems or obstacles, but in many cases, sharing how that dilemma in life was used to create the success they now experience!

Some of the stories are remarkable: how Mel Tillis overcame the rejection involved around his stuttering problem; how Billy Barty faced life as a "little person"; how Kenny Stabler beat the prejudice against left-handed quarterbacks; how Sally Jessy Raphael rose above eighteen different firings before landing her position as talk-show host; how Warren Moon got caught stealing as a fourteen-year-old, and even how

Amy Grant dealt with an autograph session early in her career when nobody showed up!

Coping with the rejection or the prejudice or the police or the empty room made them stronger people in their inner resolve. These were the stories of the potter smashing the jar in more modern times. Life is more than determination, but these experiences clearly had a molding effect on some well-known folks.

Because it is so deeply embedded in my personality, I guess I will always struggle with control. And therefore, I guess I will always be the kind of person that feels loss intensely. But I can say that I am now at a place where I am seeking to bring my "control under control." I see now that I am not endearing myself to anyone through seeking to run his or her life. God continues to teach me about my need to be a lump of clay, moldable in His hands for whatever shape He chooses.

I am also learning the value of being a shovel as opposed to a jar. Where I was once haughty, proud, and even sometimes arrogant, I am feeling the Refiner's fire ever burning away those tendencies in my life.

Fire separates the gold from the dross. Those of us who are taking the heat often wonder, "How long must I stay under His divine torch?" In answer to that question, someone has observed, "When the gold is pure enough so that He can see His face reflected in it, He will turn down the heat."

So remember, it is God who controls the temperature.

CHAPTer 6

There Is Always Purpose

IN PAIN

I cry tears to you, Lord, tears because I cannot speak. Words are lost among my fears, pain, sorrows, losses, hurts, but tears You understand, my wordless prayer You hear. Lord, wipe away my tears, all tears, not in distant day, but now here.

—*Joe Bayly*

When my oldest son, Jesse, was still a toddler, he used to love to play hide-and-seek. He'd beg his mom or his sister or me to play with him, and when he finally got a taker, he always insisted on being the one to hide first. And usually we would humor him.

I can still remember closing my eyes and counting to fifty, assuming Jesse was running as fast as his two-year-old legs could take him. I envisioned him hiding his little body in some crevice of our small apartment, maybe behind the floor-length curtains made of that ugly green material, or under one of the beds, nestled between the storage boxes and the dust bunnies. I was always surprised when I finished counting, opened my eyes, and found Jesse still standing directly next to me by the brown-plaid couch in the apartment's biggest room—the living room.

What I came to discover was that, in his mind, Jesse *was* hiding. How? By placing his two little hands over his own eyes!

Obviously his mental process went something like this: "I can't see Daddy, so I guess he can't see me either."

I found this to be highly amusing, and I looked forward to the times he would ask me to play the game with him. I didn't have the heart to tell him about his misconception concerning our game. So I guess if I had been the only person he ever played hide-and-seek with, he would still be using the same strategy when it came time for him to find his own hiding place. That would be pretty silly for a seventeen-year-old.

But somewhere along the line, Jesse ventured out into hide-and-seek with people beyond our family. The "hands over the eyes" routine ended quickly. He probably used it only once. When the other kids found him right away, they more than likely laughed at him, made fun of his foolishness, and probably hurt his feelings. But through that experience he learned an important lesson he may have otherwise missed.

Between the toddler years and the adult years, most

of us have felt the intensity of the pain increase. We long for the days when the strongest pain was that of teasing from our peers. The pain of an adult crisis or catastrophe has raised pain's threshold to just about the pinnacle. We get to the point where we feel we can't take much more.

But there is good news even in the midst of life's most intense pain . . . there is a reason for our pain, a purpose that makes it an experience worth enduring and even positive. It was Jonathan Edwards who wisely said, "What can I learn so I won't need to go through it again?"

As I am starting to see the light once again, having come through the dark days of my personal crisis, I am continually seeing more brightly the lessons God wants me to learn, based on what I went through. This entire book represents much of what I am learning. Here are several key concepts in my life:

THERE IS PRACTICAL VALUE IN TEARS

As if God sensed I needed to be more contemporary, to be more "with it," to become more of a '90s guy, He convinced me of the value of tears. I have always thought of myself as a sensitive male, a caring, nurturing type; however, I was never one for tears, *especially* if there were other people around.

When we watched a movie or television show together as a family, I can still remember diverting my eyes from the children so they would not see me cry at a sad portion of the show. The standing joke around our house was that I hated all shows about animals, since they most always, in the tradition of *Old Yeller,* died at the end. Therefore, I steadfastly refused to watch any animal adventures.

I don't know if it was a male thing or a Northeastern thing or an individual personality thing, but when my crisis hit, I was left with no other alternative but to turn over a completely new leaf.

For a guy who had never cried before, I was suddenly crying rivers. On quite a few occasions I cried so long and so hard that I depleted the water supply in my tear ducts. Just like a person gets the dry heaves, I experienced the dry cries. I was so devastated by my tragedy, there was no other way to express it.

And as I was to learn, that's what tears are for.

Several months after I was single again, I was at my desk working on one of my ghostwriting projects when the phone rang. Picking it up, I heard the voice of a friend on the other end.

"Bill? This is Norm Wright. How are you doing? I just heard about your situation and I'm calling to let you know I care about you. Is there anything I can do to help you as you process some of this stuff?"

I was somewhat shocked by what I was hearing. Norm and I had worked together on just a few occasions when we were sharing the platform at some sort of conference. I considered him a friend, but his tone on the phone made me feel like his long-lost buddy.

"Gee, Norm, I don't know what to say," I fumbled. "I'm flattered that you would think enough of me to call me and offer to help."

"You've helped a lot of people in your ministry, Bill—especially families," Norm remarked. "It's going to be wonderful to see how this crisis will open up new doors for you as you continue to help others."

I was dumbfounded by these last remarks. I had felt pretty much like a player who got benched for a foul. I hadn't given much consideration to being invited off the bench to join the game again.

"Bill, I've got a book of mine I want to send you," Norm continued. "I've come through my own time of grief and loss. I hope you'll find it helpful and comforting."

I always knew Norm as an extremely prolific writer, so I had no idea which of his more than forty books he was planning on sending.

What I received a few days later was his 1993 work, *Recovering from the Losses of Life*. Sure enough, Norm and his wife, Joyce, had just come through the death of their son, Matthew. He died at twenty-two years of age, profoundly mentally retarded. The Wrights told their story with openness, honesty, and vulnerability. This little paperback became a book of great help to me. I needed only to arrive at the third chapter when

I stumbled over a couple of phrases that put on paper what I had been struggling to make sense of for weeks. The chapter is entitled "The Meaning of Grief," and the quote had to do with crying: "Tears are the vehicle that God has equipped us with to express the deepest feelings words cannot express."[1] Then using a quote from my friend Max Lucado, Norm made the idea even more cogent and concise: "The principle is simple; when words are most empty, tears are most apt."[2]

That was it! The lightbulb went on in my head. For these long, arduous months, I was expressing something that could not be articulated in words. I was crying, weeping, blubbering—all the conceivable synonyms available for describing the shedding of tears.

And in that brief moment I finally understood why. There was so much bottled up (good word choice) inside of me that needed a chance to come out. With that dawning of knowledge came a radical transformation . . . I now cry freely, anytime, anywhere. I mean it. Ask my kids, they've sure seen the change.

Whereas my kids used to warn me about certain movies they had seen that they didn't think I would like, now they warn me about certain movies they know will make me cry. It's kind of their way of saying, "Dad, I know you'll start blubbering at this one, so if you don't want to make a spectacle of yourself at the theater, you might want to wait until this one is available on video, and you can rent it and weep in the privacy of your own family at home." Oh, those thoughtful kids of mine!

I specifically remember Jesse seeing the movie *Mrs. Doubtfire* at our local theater. He came home and issued me a stern warning, "Don't go see it, Dad. It's all about divorce and child custody and that kind of stuff. It'll get to you. Wait until it hits the video stores and spare yourself the embarrassment."

I appreciated his concern, but I also started getting phone calls from friends, asking me if I had seen this flick. I became immensely curious and so, one night, I snuck out to catch the ten o'clock show.

Jesse was right. I cried at the beginning, I cried at the middle, I cried at the end. "I thought Robin Williams was supposed to be funny!" I'd moan to myself as I tried to regain my composure. "I'm so fortunate to have my kids," I'd add, as the waterworks would begin all over again.

Those crying times would leave me exhausted and completely drained. Oftentimes I would be the very last person in the theater trying to put myself back together so I could leave with some degree of decorum. I became a real connoisseur of closing credits. I knew all the theater staff by first name.

And yet, through it all, I look back on those experiences with a measure of satisfaction for what I was able to express through those silent seasons of tears. I needed it for my heart like I needed oxygen for my lungs.

There are quite a few references to me crying in this book, and now you know that it was not always that way for me. It was a valuable lesson I learned through pain, and I am thankful to God for it.

There were more lessons to learn as well.

THE PRINCIPLE OF BEING PROACTIVE

Like hundreds of thousands of other Americans, somewhere along the line I picked up a copy of Stephen Covey's mega-blockbuster, *The Seven Habits of Highly Effective People*.[3] And, like many people, I allowed it to sit on a shelf, untouched and unread for many months. I just never got around to it. I hate to think of all the other books that collect dust on my shelves, still left unread.

Once I hit my crisis, however, and suddenly faced six months without work, I had some extra time on my hands to get around to a lot of things I never was able to before. So I picked up the book and began to read.

What started as skimming quickly evolved into poring. With my journal by my side, I labored over every sentence in the book, recording page after page of minute detail concerning my thoughts on how it specifically related to me—particularly how it applied to me during this time of crisis.

The first habit espoused by Covey is to be proactive.

Stated briefly, it means that between stimulus and response in human beings lies the power to choose. Proactivity, then, means that we are solely responsible for what happens in our lives. No fair blaming anyone or anything else. Period.

I found this principle to be of great help to me. I didn't take it to be in contradiction to the hand of God, but rather an extension of it. God allowed these circumstances to occur, and I would be getting nowhere by centering my time around blaming someone for my woes.

This was an easy temptation to give in to, especially since it was specifically a divorce that was the focus of my crisis. The most common human tendency is to lash out and blame the former spouse for every imaginable evil ever committed in the marriage. "I wouldn't be in this mess if it wasn't for her!" This is, unfortunately, a phrase I had uttered on numerous occasions up to that point.

But reading those words brought me to the point of self-confrontation. *You can sit here day after day, wallowing in self-pity, blaming everybody and his uncle for your catastrophe, or you can get up off your fat duff and start the process of rebuilding your life. You've got to stop living in this "victim scenario." Take responsibility for what is yours and learn to let go of the rest of it.*

The more I read Covey, the more I saw that proactivity was all about *response*. It's not what happens to us, but how we respond to what happens to us. That was not new information to me, but it set differently this time around.

I was in a real downward spiral in my responses. I was angry, hurt, bitter, and filled with despair. *Is this how you want to teach your kids to respond to life?* I asked myself, knowing full well the correct answer. *Do you want them to see a man who has utterly succumbed to the outside pressures? Is there no inner core of faith that can sustain you during this time of pain? Are you teaching your kids to just give in and be victims when they're knocked down? What lessons of character are you passing on?*

This issue of what I was communicating to my kids was a sensitive one with me. I had been noticing that the kids were becoming somewhat uncomfortable with me in my deepest stages of self-pity and victimization. It started to feel like they were with me more out of duty than desire.

The more I thought about it, I couldn't blame them. What kid would want to be around a middle-aged, fuddy-duddy who sat around all day and night moping, weeping, and feeling sorry for himself?

Looking back, I believe God used a combination of all these factors to bring me out of my lethargy. I also believe that it was all in God's perfect timing. Coming out of it any quicker would have allowed for too short of a grieving period, and wallowing in it any longer would have allowed for too long of one.

I have a friend who went through a vocational crisis

who relates perfectly to the need for proactivity. When his business went under, Ryan, like any other person who would endure a crisis of this nature, became almost paralyzed for a period of time. He recalled the feeling of utter and complete despair.

"I didn't want to get out of bed in the morning," Ryan remembered. "Life as I had known it had ground to a total halt. I felt that all purpose and meaning in life had run away. I can still recall hearing the alarm, turning it off, and rolling over with the covers pulled way up over my head."

But ultimately Ryan discovered that he couldn't live the rest of his life as a victim. "I began taking some personal responsibility for the rebuilding of my life. I initiated some conversations with a guy who would eventually become my partner. Before long, we had a new business conceived that we could operate from the basement of my house right here in Shreveport.

"Then the real healing began. I had spent just about my entire adult life behind a desk in an office, but I had always had this secret urge to work construction. I was a weekend home-improvement guy who had all kinds of tools that were my all-time favorite toys. So I decided that, since my basement needed to be completely remodeled into office space, rather than pay a professional to do it, *I'd* do it!

"What I had expected to take place did in fact occur." Ryan smiled as he recollected, "I found tremendous catharsis in the daily activity of sawing wood, hanging drywall, plumbing, painting, and doing all the finish work. No longer did I turn off the alarm and roll over—I was waking up *before* the alarm went off!"

Looking down at his hands, he added, "I remember telling my wife, Mitzi, to pray for these. I felt that if I injured my hands, obviously I wouldn't be able to finish my construction. And that bothered me, because it also meant that I wouldn't be able to finish the work that was going on inside of me at the time. I was taking responsibility for what was mine and the Lord was healing me in the process. Thankfully, God was gracious, because I was able to finish . . . in every sense of the word.

"It's Covey's principle of proactivity," Ryan summarized. "The smartest day of my business career was the day I stopped blaming so-and-so for running us out of business and took responsibility for the rebuilding of a new life."

As for the principles I am learning and presenting in this book, take them all together. Proactivity doesn't override the need to grieve, for example. Time and distance provide perspective, and it's most often after that perspective has returned that proactivity can thrive in a life.

THE FELLOWSHIP OF SUFFERINGS

Humility has kept me from putting this following

story in print, but enough time has passed to cause a level of comfort in sharing it.

I was a member of the Miami Dolphins organization in 1972–1973.

Those of you who are up to speed on your NFL trivia will immediately recognize that as the season we went 17-0, the only perfect season in the long and rich history of the National Football League.

Coach Shula knew me for my strong throwing arm, my awesome side-to-side agility, and my speed. My position?

I sold programs that season at the Orange Bowl!

Being a program salesman may not sound as glorious as positions held by Bob Griese, Larry Csonka, or Mercury Morris, but I assure you I was a valuable member of the Dolphin family.

Like my teammates on the field, a program salesman needed to arrive at the ballpark early in order to prepare for the game. If we had a 1 P.M. kickoff, it was not uncommon for program salesmen to be already in position in the hot, south Florida sunshine by 9 A.M. Rookies would find their positions in the park, while seasoned veterans like myself would man our posts in the more coveted position—outside the park—thus being the first program salesmen in line. We all knew that buying a program once you were in the stadium was less intentional and more of an afterthought.

"Programs here!" we'd bark. "Get your red-hot

programs. You can't tell who the players are without a program!"

Often we'd be at the Orange Bowl so early, there was no fan action whatsoever. Usually, on those days, we'd all congregate in a section of the stadium to watch the activities on the field. Players, still not in their game uniforms, would be passing or kicking or punting or running patterns.

On the last home game of that season, as we program salesmen sat quietly in our nosebleed section of the stands at the Orange Bowl, we watched as an army of young boys marched out onto the field. Dressed in uniforms that were exact miniatures of the pros', they were all part of the Punt, Pass, and Kick Competition sponsored by Ford Motor Company. It didn't take long for us to deduce that they were being coached on how to compete for the passing part of the contest, which was normally held at halftime. Back in those days, before the television halftime shows, the networks televised the competition as a live part of their game festivities.

The TV director was showing the boys one by one the line they would run up to. Then, he imitated a passing movement with his right arm, followed by hustling back to the end of the line in order to keep the contest moving. We laughed at some of the participants, simply because they were so tiny. From where we were sitting, the youngest child looked like an ant suited up in a Miami Dolphin's uniform.

After the instructions were given, we watched the assistant directors lead the kids off the field in single file. A buddy of mine pointed out the smallest of the contestants, who had become separated from the rest of the line. Quickly it became apparent that it was intentional, for he wanted the green grass of the Orange Bowl all to himself. As the last of the children exited the kid got his wish.

All by himself, with no idea the program salesmen were watching him, this kid let his fantasy kick in. He had always wanted to be the star of the game, and as the only real player in his imaginary game, he was a superstar.

He ran to the middle of the fifty-yard line and bent his knees slightly. He had both his hands, one over the other, right in front of him and his head began bobbing back and forth. We quickly figured out he was a quarterback, lined up behind his center, calling the signals and awaiting the snap.

Soon the imaginary ball was hiked from between the legs of the imaginary center. The kid started back into the pocket, looking for his favorite receiver. But there was trouble. Apparently the imaginary offensive line was weak, because soon our hero was being chased out of the pocket, forced to scramble by the imaginary defensive blitz. It was hilarious to watch this little kid, in his Dolphin's helmet and jersey, weaving back and forth from one side of the field to the other, still looking for a receiver in his imaginary game. Finally there was a breakthrough on the far end of the field.

Our quarterback cocked his right arm and let go of a pass that was an imaginary bomb down the left side of the field. Right before our very eyes, the scene magically changed. Our little quarterback was miraculously transfigured into a new position . . . he was now an all-pro wide receiver!

This squirt was now sprinting all out down the left side of the field. Next thing we knew, he leaped and pulled in the imaginary pass. Then he continued his sprint toward the end zone about thirty yards away. But, once again, this child had a very active imagination, because he was being pursued by an inordinate amount of defensive players. The opposing team must have emptied their bench, 'cause this receiver was high-stepping and dodging one defender after another, running down the field in anything but a straight line.

The boy soon realized the climax of his fantasy by running over the end zone and scoring his imaginary touchdown. Back in 1972, spiking the ball, dancing a jig, doing the twist, or a series of cartwheels were all still allowed by the NFL, and this kid did them all. He was in his own world, happy as a lark for having won his imaginary game.

With the best of intentions, all of us program salesmen stood to our feet and cheered the kid with all the gusto we could muster. But, like I said, the little boy had no idea he was being watched and as soon as we started to cheer, he became completely embarrassed and sort of crawled into his helmet and rolled it off the field.

I've never forgotten that little boy because he has been the perfect example of someone who thought he was in the game when it was really just all in his mind. It is never as easy as it was for that kid. The enemy is not imaginary, he is real. You can't simply dodge every defender, for eventually one of them will catch up to you and lay you out on the ground like a pancake.

Now I don't want to make this story stand for more than it should, but I have given this illustration much thought in recent days. For a long time, I felt I was an active part of the real game, and I guess in many ways I really was a player.

But, as I have stated, I never had a crisis of any magnitude in my life until the failure of my marriage. And so, in that way, I was a player in a much easier game, more like the kid by himself on the Orange Bowl turf.

Now I am a player in a real contest. In a sense I have joined a better team, an elite corps of crack troops ready to bang heads against an enemy that is real! It's the realization of Paul's phrase: "That I may know Him, and the power of His resurrection and the fellowship of His sufferings, being conformed to His death."[4]

I am now not only part of a group of people who know Him, and the power of His resurrection, but also a part of that specially recruited division that personally understands the fellowship of His sufferings. Three years ago, I could only speculate what that must mean, and now I can articulate it with greater ease.

I imagine you can too. There's something about the bond I have encountered since I have started sharing about my period of pain. The divorcee understands the pain, as does the parent who lost a child to death. It's a pain understood and felt by the quadriplegic and the person who lost his life's savings when his business went under. That fellowship extends to the middle-aged woman who thought her marriage would be stronger at this point in her life, and the thirty-four-year-old single lady who is uncomfortable accepting her singleness as permanent.

So, for you who read these words, who are also a part of this brigade of special forces, I say in total candor that I am honored to be in your midst. It is a privilege to serve with such a uniquely qualified group. These last few years have opened my eyes to the people closest to God Himself.

And the records are clear. God has big plans for us. That's why our tribe has increased as it has. There's purpose in all the pain we have been called to endure. We're no longer little kids playing an imaginary game. You and I have been chosen to be in that select group that will play the real game.

What's really exciting is that, like many of you, I've read the playbook. I know the outcome of the game . . . God wins.

CHAPTer 7

God Is
the
GREAT HEALER

*There is always an easy solution to every human problem—
neat, plausible, and wrong.*

—H. L. Mencken

I'd have to say I've been pretty fortunate
when it comes to medical matters. At forty-
two years of age, I've never broken a bone in my body,
never required a single stitch, never used the emergency room, and with the exception of getting my
wisdom teeth pulled, never been hospitalized. Besides
an occasional skinned knee as a kid, I came out pretty
unscathed.

To keep this amazing story alive, all five of my kids
are just about as fortunate. There have been some
stitches and some emergency room visits, but no broken bones and amazingly fine health overall. When I
think of what I have dodged in the way of medical bills,
I bow down in utter thanksgiving to God.

Certainly I am proud of my clean bill of health, but

I have observed an evil side effect that is associated with this physical wholeness. When I *do* get sick, I am the biggest baby you've ever seen.

THE NEED FOR HEALING

I think I really perfected the big-baby syndrome during my college years. I grew up in Philadelphia but went all the way to Miami, Florida, to attend college. Since this was my first time away from home, getting sick was the perfect opportunity to wallow in self-pity and bask in low self-esteem.

Once, during my sophomore year in college, I came down with a case of the flu. I want to say it was a bad case of the flu, but I was such a baby, it was probably a very mild case. I had a fever, some achy muscles, a minor sore throat, a slightly stuffed nose, and my eyes burned. Millions of us have endured this sort of twenty-four-hour virus a dozen or more times in our lifetimes. No big deal.

Except when it was me. I could make the flu into the bubonic plague. Feeling the early symptom of chills, I hustled to the college health-services office for some medication. Fortunately for me, my favorite nurse Shirley was on duty, a cute little gal with gorgeous blonde hair and a lovely smile that showed perfect white teeth. I particularly liked Shirley because she would feel sorry for me when I was sick. She'd make sad eyes and groan when I explained how my entire body was racked with excruciating pain. I have no idea why she was so nice to me, but it sure felt good. I loved the attention I received from her . . . I guess I actually craved it.

"Shirley, I'm sick." I choked out the words as if they were my last.

"What's wrong?"

"I think I'm getting the flu," I said with the same sort of severity that would have normally accompanied a statement like, "I think I have cancer."

Shirley nodded understandingly, smiled lovingly at me, and proceeded to take my temperature. My head was on fire so I was certain it would register in the 104-105-degree range. So you can imagine my amazement when she reported, "Well, you do have a slight fever . . . 100 degrees."

"What should I do?" I asked, waiting for her to call 911 for a rescue unit to transport me to intensive care.

"Go up to your dorm room and go to bed," she stated, turning her attention to filling in the student health form resting on her Plexiglas clipboard.

"That's all?" I replied incredulously.

"Take some aspirin—two every four hours, drink some orange juice, and sleep. It's very important that you do as I say. My guess is that by this time tomorrow you'll be feeling much better."

I glanced at my watch. Ten-thirty A.M. That meant I could get out of class today and tomorrow! Then I realized I had the worst timing in the world. "Today's Friday, right?" I suddenly blurted out.

"That's right."

"Oh that's just great," I moaned sarcastically.

"What's the problem?"

"Well, first of all, with tomorrow being Saturday, and having no classes on Saturday, I'll only miss one day of class. That's today. But there's an even bigger problem . . . tonight's Friday night and I have a date. I can't break my date. It'll be all right if I go, won't it?"

"That's up to you," Shirley replied. "But if I were you, I'd get my rest so I felt better by the end of the weekend."

Putting on the sad little puppy-dog face I had rehearsed for hours in front of the bathroom mirror, I moped out of the health office and poked up the stairs to my dorm room. Having a room in the same building as the health office was really convenient, and it made possible this wonderful Academy Award-winning exit from the nurse's office after each visit. Those around me were truly moved by my performances.

Once upstairs, I decided I had better listen to Shirley. My roommate came in as I was preparing to go to bed around 11 A.M. I told him of my debilitating illness and reluctantly asked him to get the word to my date for the evening. This was really killing me, since I had so few dates in college. I felt I just couldn't afford to miss any due to illness.

Closing the drapes so it was completely dark, I climbed into bed and slept for eight hours. When I awoke, it was a little after seven in the evening and I was burning up with fever. The sheets were soaked, as were all my bedclothes.

I called out for my roommate but he was gone. *He's out with his girlfriend,* I remembered and suddenly I was overcome with jealousy. I muttered to myself, "He gets to go out on a date, but I have to sit in this bed burning up with the worst fever any human has ever been asked to endure."

Self-pity started kicking in big time. "My fever must be close to 110," I concluded after feeling my forehead. "I'll bet it's high enough to kill me . . . I've got to get some help."

I was hallucinating. (Probably not, but it sounds good.)

"I need the nurse . . . that's it . . . I've got to get down the stairs . . . I've got to see Shirley . . . she'll help me . . . she'll heal me."

And with that I climbed out of bed. As soon as I stood up, everything started spinning and going black. My legs collapsed and I fell to the floor.

I started crawling over to the door. That's right, crawling. It was the most pathetic picture you could imagine: a twenty-year-old man crawling on all fours in a desperate attempt to be healed.

Opening my dorm door, I continued my crawl

down the hall. The dorm was empty and silent, for, as I said, it was Friday and everyone was out on dates. Everyone except me.

Eventually I arrived at the stairway. One by one, I negotiated the stairs so as not to plummet to my death. At the second landing I came face to face (actually my face was about in line with her shin) with a girl walking up the stairs. "What's wrong?" she asked with a rather carefree attitude.

"I'm sick," I replied. "I'm so sick, I think I'm going to die. I'm trying to get to the nurse's office."

At that point it dawned on her that I was a real piece of work and she offered to assist me. "You wait here. I'll go get the nurse."

I was more than willing to obey. I curled up on the landing and awaited the arrival of Shirley, knowing she would make me feel better. The very thought brought the slightest trace of a smile to my lips.

It had not yet occurred to me that Shirley was the nurse on the *day* shift. In my infatuation, I truly believed Shirley had no life outside of nursing. By this time of evening the shift change had occurred and with it, the nurse who best represented the exact opposite of Shirley was now on duty. She was every sick person's most horrible nightmare, come to life in a polyester white jumpsuit.

Regina.

Let's put it this way . . . Regina was the sort of nurse

who didn't major in bedside manner. For every ounce of understanding that Shirley could produce, Regina could manufacture a pound of cold, hard, brutal truth. A rather large woman, somewhat masculine in appearance, she could use her strength to push you around when necessary.

When Regina climbed the stairs to where I was sitting, she wasted no time in interrogating me.

"What in the world are you doing here on the stairs?" she demanded, hands on hips, tapping one foot against the stair right under my chin, which was quivering in terror.

"I'm sick. I'm so sick I think I'm going to die." I repeated the liturgy of death for her suspicious ears.

"Just what makes you think you're going to die?" she quizzed, shaking her head in disapproval.

"Feel my head," I suggested. "I'm burning up with fever. I think my temperature is high enough to do permanent brain damage and possibly kill me." I had just thought of the brain-damage angle and was feeling a little proud of myself.

Regina put her large, cold, clammy paw on my forehead and laughed out loud. "Ha! You call this a burning fever? It barely feels like it's over 100. I can't believe you're trying to pull this sort of scam."

My countenance fell. Where was Shirley when I needed her? She would have believed me. She would have nodded encouragingly as I told of my flirt with death. But Regina would have none of it.

"Go back to your room" was all she offered in the way of understanding. She had the softness of a rock slide.

"I need medicine," I pleaded as I attempted to stand to my feet.

"Listen to me, mister," Regina replied as she abruptly reached out and grabbed my shoulders. She looked like she was going to start shaking me, but even she seemed to realize that if she did that I would have tossed my cookies. So, instead, she stared directly into my eyes and looked at me as if I were an escapee from an asylum. Her look made me shudder.

"I want you to go to your room and go back to bed. You are not going to die. You are behaving like a big baby . . . so grow up!"

Regina pushed me away, spun around on the platform heels of her white nurse's shoes, and marched back down the stairs, "to take care of people who are really sick," I believe I heard her mumble. I wanted to stick out my tongue at her, but I was afraid she'd see me.

I still felt the need to crawl up the stairs, but I knew that while I was in Regina's field of vision, it was important for me to walk upright. Exacting my own level of personal revenge, however, I decided to mumble something myself, making sure the sound of my voice penetrated the stairway: "I wish Shirley were here. . . . I need someone to heal me."

A MORE CONTEMPORARY TALE OF HEALING

In many ways I have never outgrown that need for healing. For most of my adult life it was fairly invisible, but when my crisis realigned the structure of my life, I once again cried out to be healed. The main difference was that this time the need was genuine. It was not a tale of self-pity, though I experienced that at times, too, but a story of real pain.

And the other difference was, I didn't need Shirley. I needed God.

I've been very fortunate over the last six years to have my pastor and my best friend be the same person. Ed Neuenschwander and I go back to the early days of the *Insight for Living* radio ministry in southern California. *Insight for Living* is the radio ministry of Chuck Swindoll. Chuck and I had been friends for a long time and I jumped at the opportunity to work with him. I can still remember being flown out to Fullerton from south Florida to interview for the job of counseling associate. Rhonda and I spent a fair amount of time with the Swindolls, but we were also introduced to this couple with the unusually long last name. I would be reporting to Ed, so it made sense that I was supposed to get to know my new boss. We immediately hit it off with Ed and Candee, and they even drove us around town in their van, pointing out which neighborhoods were the most desirable in our price range. Miraculously, with no money and a 17 percent interest rate mortgage, we bought our first home.

My earliest memories of Ed are of a focused, fun-loving, family man who immediately treated me as an equal even though he was my boss. For that first year we worked together, Ed would swing by and pick me up every morning so that Rhonda could have use of our car. Things like this car pool helped me get to know Ed even better. For example, it was this routine that helped me discover one of Ed's quirks in life . . . he never goes to work the identical way two days in a row. What was for most folks a predictable fifteen-minute jaunt down the major streets in town would turn into an adventure, often worthy of Indiana Jones status. He knew all the back roads in every part of Orange County, and it wasn't long before, like it or not, I was learning them too.

The staff in our office counseled hundreds of folks by mail and phone. Ed and I put together a string of correspondence that offered hope and encouragement to Chuck's listeners. We also contributed to the writing of the Bible study guides that accompanied the broadcasts. Between Ed and me, we cranked out dozens of those babies.

Our office was right across the street from a great

Mexican restaurant. In an effort to increase business, they advertised a Mexican breakfast, served from 7 A.M. until 11 A.M. To further entice customers, several of the breakfasts dishes were only ninety-nine cents. With the added incentive of free baskets of chips and bowls of salsa, this was a meal deal that couldn't be beaten.

In order to further maximize the eating experience on a budget, Ed and I used to wait until 10:59 A.M. and then go over there for an early lunch! Those are fond memories of the two of us, scarfing chips and salsa, solving the world's problems, and dreaming of the day when we'd be off to ministry adventures of our own. To this day, whenever I get indigestion, I think of the future.

Ed's adventure took off before mine did. In 1985, Ed and Candee were invited to take the pastorate of a church located eight hours north of us in a little town I had never heard of—Grass Valley. Nestled in the Sierra foothills, it was a picturesque town and a wonderful opportunity for my fellow worker.

We bid a tearful good-bye, never imagining that three short years later, I would move my entire family to the same little town, and we'd once again become neighbors and friends. But this time there was an added dimension I had not previously experienced . .

Ed was now the senior pastor of the church we chose to attend.

Ed and Candee often opened their home to us.

They even invited us to join them for the most festive of occasions, Thanksgiving and Christmas dinner. Few people set a table with more grace and elegance than Candee. Often we reciprocated with a little New Year's Eve blast, but as the years flew by, I increasingly found it more and more difficult to stay up until midnight.

I still remember one particular Christmas evening we were all together at their home. After we ate, we played games until the wee hours of the morning. As we prepared to leave, someone looked out the window to discover it had been steadily snowing and freezing over the streets while we had been happily distracted inside. So, in order to avoid the icy roads, Candee brought out sleeping bags, air mattresses, and comforters, so the seven Butterworths could settle in for a night's rest at the home of their friends. By the time we awoke, the warm rays of the morning's sun had caused the ice to disappear.

Those next few years were hectic ones for me. I worked hard to establish myself on the speaking circuit, and so when I was in town, I usually spent the time with my family. Therefore the time I spent with Ed was fairly minimal. It's amazing to me, as I look back on those times, that Ed hung in there with me and loved me even when I had little time to spend with him. He's just that kind of guy.

As things began to unravel in my personal life, I found myself pulling away from Ed. Between embarrassment, confusion, and utter despair, I wrongly chose to isolate myself from those who could reach out to help me. Several months went by before I could scrounge up enough courage to tell Ed of my catastrophe. When I finally made the phone call, it was a matter of *seconds* before I found myself thinking, *Why have I waited so long to tell such a good friend?*

Ed and I started spending more time together. He was helpful as a listener, a shoulder to cry on, and a supporting encourager. I remember crying with him on numerous occasions . . . in his home, at the church in his study, in his car, on the steps of his front porch, and even over the phone.

THE HEALING HAND OF GOD

Another aspect of our relationship began to have a beneficial effect on me as well. Unlike any other time in our friendship, I was marveling at what I was learning from Ed from the pulpit on Sunday mornings. He had always been good, but at that point he became almost *extraordinary*. Many a Sunday morning I would leave the sanctuary with a renewed sense of God's hand in what was happening in my life. Even though I couldn't explain why I was going through what I was going through, I was seeing that God in His love would ultimately provide the healing of my soul.

Without question, a real turning point for me in my spiritual journey came the Sunday of the first Christmas I was single again. What had always been the highlight of the year, December 25, was now an awkward occasion of negotiating "who had whom" from "when to when" and how to best handle the minutiae of keeping Christmas special to the kids when inside I was a brokenhearted wreck.

As I walked into the sanctuary that Sunday before Christmas, the room was warmly decorated with wreaths and ribbons and lanterns. The central focus, however, was a life-size manger, placed on the floor in front of the pulpit. Real straw was brimming from the four sides of the manger, and it wonderfully re-created what the Christ-child must have lain in on that cold winter's night.

When Ed stood up to preach that morning, I had already wept quietly several times as we sang a procession of well-known Christmas carols. Each song was pregnant with memories of Christmases past, when everything in the world was so much better.

I wonder what Ed will say this year? I found myself thinking before he began. I've always felt Christmas and Easter are tough preaching assignments for a pastor, not because the message is difficult, but because the congregation expects him to come at the same story from a different angle every year! There are only so many ways you can find meaning in gold, frankincense, and myrrh, for example, and no room at the inn only can go so far in its practical application.

Therefore, Ed chose to go deeper into Luke's gospel account, later in the life of Christ. He chose as his text a verse from the fourth chapter, when Jesus was actually a grown man. But it was a verse that was especially relevant to the Christmas season. It read:

> The Spirit of the LORD is upon Me,
> Because He anointed Me to preach the gospel to the poor.
> He has sent Me to proclaim release to the captives,
> And recovery of sight to the blind,
> To set free those who are downtrodden.[1]

Ed went on to explain that this was actually a quote from the Old Testament. Isaiah had spoken these words centuries before in prophecy of the coming Messiah. In Isaiah it reads this way:

> The Spirit of the Lord GOD is upon me,
> Because the LORD has anointed me
> To bring good news to the afflicted;
> He has sent me to bind up the brokenhearted,
> To proclaim liberty to captives,
> And freedom to prisoners.[2]

When Ed finished reading Isaiah's words, it was as if there was no longer anyone else in the worship service. I felt as if he were speaking directly to me and me alone. He chose to zero in on a key phrase—"He sent me to bind up the brokenhearted."

"Is this year a difficult Christmas for you?" Ed asked. "Are you brokenhearted over a circumstance that has left you in great pain?"

Tears were streaming down my cheeks as I knew that this was a message from God for me. All that moisture dripping down onto my lap was silently answering Ed, "Yes . . . yes . . . I am brokenhearted."

Meanwhile Ed had moved from his position behind the pulpit to a place in front of it. Standing over the manger, he crouched down and said, "If you're here in deep pain, I want you to do something for me. I invite you to leave your burden here in the manger. For remember, Jesus Christ has come to mend that which is torn inside of you. He has come to bind up your broken heart."

I don't remember much of what happened after that, except that in my soul, I gave Christ all the pain my crisis had created. It wasn't the sort of thing that was accompanied by harps, strings, or chills up the spine, but it was an awesomely moving encounter for me. In many ways, it was like nothing I had ever experienced.

Christmas was bearable, thanks to Him who had come to bind up my broken heart. I was so grateful that I had made this discovery at what could have been the most awful time of the year. God was loving me, healing me, and giving me strength. In God's great timing, He was allowing me to experience a spiritual high.

A DAILY REMINDER

As the New Year arrived, I was earnestly trying to accept my new position in life and move on to the new dimensions awaiting me. Many positive things happened in that time period, but there were also times of continued struggle.

For example, I battled mightily with loneliness. I wasn't very comfortable with my singleness and it seemed like every day there was some sort of reminder of my life as a married person. I heard a song on the radio that used to be a favorite of Rhonda's and mine. In a crowd of people, I would suddenly catch the passing scent of a perfume that was the one she had always worn. An item on a menu, a commercial on television, the slightest little thing could set me off on painful nostalgia.

Of particular pain for me was the early morning alarm's sound to announce another new day. I would turn off the alarm quickly, so as to not disturb anyone else. As I would roll over, I would once again realize there was no one else in this bed to disturb. The other side was empty. To make it worse, the other side of the bed was flanked by a nightstand, once brimming with books and tissues and magazines and knickknacks, now utterly naked.

It was the empty nightstand that brought a lump to my throat at the start of every day. Its bareness silently testified to my pain. But God, the Great Healer, could bind my broken heart even in its daily despair.

What happened occurred quite innocently, after New Year's, around the time we were putting all the Christmas decorations away for another year. I quietly took down the tree and the tinsel and the lights. As I was about to box up the tiny nativity scene that traditionally graced a table in the living room, a thought occurred to me. I decided not to place it in its box, but to give it a different year-round home instead. Carefully I moved the nativity scene to a place where it could be loved and cherished . . . on top of the empty nightstand by my bed.

It is still there to this day. That night table is no longer a plain of pain and loneliness. It is now a place brimming with the symbols of renewal and hope. Every morning when I awake, I roll over and glance across my bed to see the little baby Jesus in His tiny manger. And I remember: He has come to heal the brokenhearted.

PARt THREE

Putting the Pieces Back Together

CHAPT*er* 8

The Many Facets of a Healthy **IDENTITY**

The most cheerful people I have met, with few exceptions, have been those who had the least sunshine and the most pain and suffering in their lives.

—*M. R. DeHaan, M.D.*

I fly a lot and I've learned over the last few years that the flight attendants really are there for my safety.

For those of us who log thousands of air miles a year, we've probably gotten to the place where we can recite from memory the safety speech that the flight attendants give before every takeoff. We know how to buckle the seat belt low and tight across our laps. We know where the nearest emergency exits are—we can even point to them with two fingers from each hand. We know our seat is a flotation device, and we know how to hug it closely to our chests. We also know it is a violation of federal law to disarm or in any way tamper with the smoke detectors in the lavatories.

But it's the whole spiel concerning the oxygen masks that has caught my attention in recent days. It's not the part about the bag not inflating, even though oxygen will be flowing. It's not the elastic bands that will adjust so the mask will fit snugly across your nose and mouth. It's the line where the attendant states: "If you are traveling with someone who needs assistance, *put on your mask first*, then help those around you."

Many of us in the helping professions are somewhat guilty of breaking this law of safety and survival. Teachers, pastors, counselors, social workers, missionaries, personnel officers, human resource people—any people-person runs the risk of blacking out in the middle of this flight we call life because we've given so much attention to assisting others with their oxygen masks, we've neglected to put on our own. What can appear to some as noble, is in reality, quite stupid.

For me, it took a circumstance of crisis proportions for God to get my attention on this issue. I was so busy looking out for everyone else's interests—my clients, the audiences at my speeches, my wife, my kids—I gave precious little time to the nurturing of my own soul. Nothing is sadder in life than an anorexic soul.

I was relatively blind to this whole abuse. In a rather haughty way, I was smugly observing how so many of my peers were completely wrapped up in their careers, whereas I had the wisdom to see that this was wrong. However, in a complete pendulum shift, I wrapped my life completely around my family, and specifically my wife. It never even dawned on me that if I ever lost my wife, I would be in the exact same situation that my friends would be in if they lost their jobs.

Therefore, when Rhonda wanted her new life, it hit me hard. This was the most important aspect of my life—in many respects the *only* aspect of my life—and it was disappearing with a series of legal papers.

It was several months after the fact that I came to the realization that what I needed was to redefine who I was. I needed the development of a healthy identity, and health came through many facets.

FREE THERAPY

I made this personal discovery through a consulting job for which I was employed shortly after my divorce finalized. An old friend of mine was putting together a series of presentations on healthy relationships and, as was his custom, he gathered a few trusted colleagues together to brainstorm on his proposed topics. Through this meeting, he would walk away with greater depth in his content as well as supporting material in the form of jokes, stories, and illustrations. I knew this was his standard method, but this was the first time he had invited me to participate in one of his think tanks.

I flew into Denver on a blustery winter day and took

149

a shuttle to the nearby airport hotel where the two-day session was being held. After I checked in, I freshened up a bit and then went to the prescribed meeting room where my old friend greeted me with a warm embrace. "It's good to see you again, brother," Stuart said as he beamed. "Let me introduce you to the other guys we'll have working with us on this project. I know you'll love every single one of them."

With that Stuart introduced me to two of his assistants and three other men who were brought in for their input. I was a little intimidated when I became aware of the team. These other three guys were all successful clinical psychologists with Ph.D.'s behind their names! True, they weren't in cardigan sweaters, hair balding and askew, sucking on pipes, and peering through thick bifocal lenses; they were, instead, quite normal-looking, friendly fellows. Still, I'll let you figure out who was there to add depth to his content and who was there for comic relief.

Thank goodness I didn't let my initial intimidation get the best of me, because I was in store for a treat most folks don't ever get to experience . . . I was in for a forty-eight-hour marathon therapy session.

And not only did I not have to pay for it—my friend paid me to be there!

Stuart laid out his topics one by one, and we offered our suggestions and insights on how to make these presentations even stronger.

One of the topics on the agenda was "Developing a Healthy Identity." I was prepared to hear these doctors talk about the most current thoughts on self-image, esteem issues, and the need for boundaries. Instead, one concept caused me to sit up and take careful notes.

"People in general and men in particular need to understand the importance of *spreading out* the areas from which they gain their identity," said one of the psychologists. They all knew about my situation and we all felt comfortable using it to enhance the discussion. So I wasn't surprised or offended when he turned to ask me a question.

"Bill, prior to your divorce, were you pretty good about spreading yourself out in a variety of areas?"

"Well, exactly what do you mean?"

"You know, things like job and mate and kids and friends and hobbies and personal growth and golf and a men's group. Did you have a lot of that already set in motion?"

"No," I whispered.

He nodded and then proceeded cautiously. "I'm not suggesting that had you done those things that your divorce wouldn't have been traumatic, but if a person has a variety of areas of interest in his or her life, it can make the loss of any one of those *less traumatic*. Much of that is just common sense."

That was a real breakthrough for me.

Just plain old common sense stood out as one of

the more profound lessons I have been learning in my new journey. If you have an object like a piece of plywood resting on two bricks, for example, and you remove one of the bricks, you will no longer have the plywood lying straight. It will be off balance. But if you have that object on three or more bricks, you could take away one and the plywood would stay in the same position it was in previously. Of course, it stands to reason the more bricks you have, the truer that illustration would be.

I am learning the value of having four or five areas in my life that provide me with my identity. Like the bricks, this provides me with a greater sense of balance. Unlike the bricks, more than five or six would probably prove counterproductive. Each person needs to arrive at his or her own list, but here are six of the keys in my progression in this area.

MY SIX IDENTITY-GROUNDERS

1. My Children

For most of us who go through some sort of loss, even family loss, there is still some part of our family that remains. If you have lost a child, you may still have other children or a spouse. If you have lost your mate, you may still have children. If you lost all your immediate family, you may still have extended family.

In my case, I still have my five children. At the writing of this book, four of them, Joy, Jesse, Jeffrey, and John are teenagers, so there are many ways I can be involved in their lives. It may be as menial as cooking dinner, helping with some homework assignment, doing laundry, or running car pool, but nevertheless it is a way to stay connected to them in their day-to-day world.

A family crisis can lead to feelings of self-doubt, even guilt, among the children, so it's very important to provide as much stability as possible for them. It's a constant challenge for me to maintain a regular dinner hour, a bedtime for the younger ones, regular church attendance, and an overall willingness to abide by the rules. It's hard sometimes, but in the long run it's worth pursuing.

I view my time with my children as more valuable than ever. To be completely honest, initially it was difficult for me to watch them go off to spend time with their mom, but I have come to see the selfish error of my thinking. Not only is it good for them to be with her, it's essential. But when they return, I admit, I always sigh and thank God silently for the opportunity to have my kids as an integral part of my life.

Obviously, at this point in my life I am unmarried, but I would hasten to add that those of you who are married need to develop the part of your identity that is named by being a husband or a wife. Investing in a spouse is a sweet experience. Studies have demonstrated over and over how husbands and wives can energize each other simply through their interaction. But your spouse can't be your whole world or provide your whole identity.

Don't misread my story, though, as a justification for pulling back in your marriage. Very few people need to gain distance from their spouses. Before anyone would arrive at that conclusion I think it would be wise to consult a counselor or a trusted friend. I'm sure there are people who may have to do that, but for the vast majority of married folks, a simple inventory of where you are in terms of overall identity can accomplish the necessary goals.

I am as pro-marriage as I have ever been. It is one of God's most intimate gifts. If it is His will for a mate to be a part of my life once again, I will honor her and treasure her for the rest of my life. But then and now, I want to find my identity in a number of relationships.

2. My Job

After being out of work for six months, I have a renewed appreciation for my job. It took a very short time for me to realize I had become far too comfortable in my previous situation.

I have been learning that I can derive a great deal of satisfaction from putting in a hard day's work. Of course, the whole point of this chapter is that *none* of these by itself would be right to build my entire life around, but nonetheless, a vocation is a healthy pursuit.

Many who experience life's disappointments find it in this area. The career has been less than expected and there is a real feeling of dissatisfaction and sadness. This is understandable, but it is also possible that this entire incident is God's way of pointing you in a different direction—a path you would never have chosen had this disappointment not occurred. Many can attest to that very fact.

Trevor was a man who knew success. He had risen fast in the company's organizational chart, and by the time he was thirty-two, he was at a level most people attain when they are closer to fifty. Trev, as he was known to his friends, was a risk-taker, there was no denying that fact, yet time after time every risk he took ended up in his favor, both in advancement and monetary wealth.

Other businesses began to offer Trevor large consulting fees to tap into his knowledge on a variety of subjects. It was while he was branching out in this way that the foundation of his business began to crumble.

"By a situation that was created through no fault of my own, my business was suddenly bankrupt," Trevor recollects. "My second in command basically ran off with all our assets. While I was completely trusting this man, he had all the business papers rewritten in a way that made his thievery perfectly legal. The best lawyers in the state just sat and shook their heads.

"It was such an empty feeling to be in that position.

It was only a matter of time until the consulting jobs dried up once my clients found out I had been duped out of everything I owned. I was washed up.

"At one point it was so bad, I went to see my pastor. I was really feeling down and he made a suggestion that I felt was rather unorthodox. He told me he understood how depressed I must feel, but I was still greatly blessed. He suggested I accompany him downtown to the Rescue Mission that he preaches at once a month. He told me he thought it might broaden my perspective on life.

"So I went. I was skeptical at first, thinking this would have little or no impact on me. But I was wrong. After the meeting, as I assisted the pastor in passing out sandwiches and coffee to these dear people, I had to excuse myself from my place in the serving line to run to the men's room. I started sobbing uncontrollably. I knew now what the pastor meant. I *did* have a lot to be thankful for, but I had taken so much for granted. That night I vowed to approach life differently."

Trevor's story was far from over. He was so moved by the ministry of this mission to homeless people in the inner city, he began to inquire about their financial situation. "We are totally dependent on generous people's contributions," the director told him. "We have no other subsidizing or grants."

As Trevor heard this story, the lights starting flashing in his head as they had in past business deals. He asked the director how much money he would need to pay a person a modest salary for raising funds. The director crunched some numbers and gave his answer to Trevor. "Then that's how much money I'll raise for you," he told the director confidently. "You just hired yourself a fund-raiser!" He shook the director's hand firmly.

And Trevor was true to his word. He started visiting a lot of his old friends from the business world and was quite successful at raising money for the mission. He experienced a new level of fulfillment.

"I also promised myself that I would work in the kitchen once every two weeks, just to stay close to the mission's purpose. It became a regular reminder of what I had to be grateful for.

"Looking back, it took the collapse of my business to bring me to a place where I was willing to explore an area of life that I had never even considered before. If you'd told me ten years ago I would be doing this sort of thing, I would have laughed in your face. Ironically, I am happier now than I have ever been, because I feel like I'm in a job that is truly helping people, in some real tangible ways, both in the immediate here and now and also with an eye toward eternity.

"My job is an important part of my life, but not all of it. I have learned the advantage of spreading out my identity in a variety of areas, and the result is that I am enjoying life more than ever before."

3. My Friends

Like so many of my generation, especially males, I gave lip service to the importance of friendships but did very little to cultivate them. This could have proved disastrous for me were it not for men who honestly loved me unconditionally and were willing to invest in me even when I was unwilling to invest much in them. My friends have a great deal to do with my story. They have so much to do with what I am learning that I have dedicated the entire next chapter to the ministry of my friends in my life.

But I'm not the only one convinced of the importance of friendship. Eugene knows the value of this commodity, for he too feels a debt of gratitude to his friends for their involvement in his life.

"I was an alcoholic for about ten years before even realizing it. Thanks to the people of Alcoholics Anonymous, I am alive and sober today.

"One of the things to come out of my involvement in their Twelve Step program is the buddy relationship I developed with Sonny. He has become a real godsend to me, although I would have never predicted it at our first meeting.

"When I first met Sonny all I could see was a guy who looked to be of a much lower economic standard and a totally different ethnicity from me. I remember thinking, *There is no way a poor black guy is gonna make any difference in my life!*

"I was totally wrong. Sonny was the first guy I ever met who didn't have an ulterior motive or hidden agenda with me. He just wanted to be my friend. I resisted it like crazy for the first three months, but his winning ways eventually wore me down. The best thing I ever did, besides quit drinking, was to let my walls of defense down and get to know this incredible human being named Sonny.

"Our friendship grew out of need at first. Both of us needed a guy to whom we could be accountable for our actions, especially if we were leaning toward a drink. I've called Sonny at all hours of the day and night from penthouses and phone booths, just to get his help in staying strong in what I knew was right for me. And I was able to help him in many similar situations through the years that followed. It's been something to see the two of us, a white man and a black man, embracing as true friends.

"But what has been really exciting is to see our bond grow deeper and deeper. We are far more than buddies who help each other when tempted to drink. Sonny has become like a soul mate to me. He has counseled me on countless issues, big and small.

"I've gotten to the place where I feel like one of those Secret Service guys you read about in the newspapers: I'd take a bullet for that guy!"

Eugene is one among many in our society today who is discovering the value of friends in his life. No matter what one may offer as an excuse for not developing deep and meaningful friendships, a person without friends is a little less a person than his counterpart with friends along the way.

4. My Hobbies

For many, just the mention of the word *hobbies* conjures up a mental picture of little boys collecting baseball cards, little girls playing with dolls, or adults who are so wealthy they have time to wile away the hours with leisurely pursuits. Yet very few of you who read these pages fit into any of those categories.

Our hobbies are another facet of our identity that brings us to a position of balance and health. I have reached the point in my life where I no longer apologize for the inclusion of hobbies in my life. I need them to stay on track.

Just to keep things interesting, I have a wide spectrum in the hobby realm. When I intentionally choose to spend time on a hobby, I may play a round of golf with a good friend. I used to think that golf was for other people because I was so bad at it (my motto was always "every club—every hole"). But one day I actually looked around at the others who were on the course, and I discovered that most were no better than I was and some were actually worse!

Another enjoyable hobby for me is one you would expect from a writer—I love to visit used-book stores.

I can spend hours gazing at shelf after shelf, especially in my favorite section, American History. If there's a large section on my favorite character, Theodore Roosevelt, I'm there for the day. I used to think that sounded so boring to others and I was pretty secretive about the whole adventure, but I have come to realize that it is a hobby of mine that truly brings me pleasure, so who cares what someone else may think? My hobbies need to please me, not somebody else!

If it's not golf or a good used book, maybe it's having a little jam session with my oldest son as we play our guitars together. Perhaps it's playing a game of racquet ball or discovering a new museum or restaurant. Whatever form the hobby takes, it is a wonderful way to enjoy yourself and to broaden your identity in the process.

5. Personal Growth

As the flight attendant instructed, I'm learning the value of putting my own mask on first. I had the tendency to allow personal growth to be a pretty low priority, so now I've tried to raise it on my list.

Things that feed my personal growth side are things like reading more frequently and more broadly. I love to read and so disciplining myself to provide time to read on a regular basis has been a helpful addition to my schedule. It may be a biography, a book by a favorite pastor, a whodunit murder mystery, an historical novel, or a theology book, but through those pages

I am transported to a place where my soul is fed and nourished.

I have always been an advocate of journaling. Through the years my journals have chronicled my path in life, both the smooth stretches of road and the rocky sections as well. The advantage that I have found in journal-keeping is that it allows me to articulate what I am feeling. Rather than always being in a mode of taking in, or having thoughts and feelings that go unexpressed, writing in a journal provides an occasion to write down exactly what's going on inside of me at a given moment.

Looking back over a journal is like walking back in time. For example, my journal has been extremely helpful in reestablishing my thoughts and feelings at the time of my crisis. Things I felt I would *never* forget, in fact, I did. The fact that those emotions have healed speaks to me of God's faithfulness.

6. Spiritual Growth

In many respects personal growth and spiritual growth overlap, but I have chosen to think of them as two separate sources for my identity. My walk with God is more focused than some of the examples I used to describe my personal growth.

For many years I taught people truths from the Bible as part of my job. I went to college and seminary for the express purpose of studying the Scriptures in greater detail. From an outsider's point of view, if anyone should have had a rich, satisfying experience with spiritual growth, it should have been me.

Yet, as many who are in similar positions will attest, it was precisely all that training and all that everyday exposure that brought a numbness to the Scriptures. The Bible could easily become a resource book for future communications, not a life-giving supply of truth. Embarrassing as it is to admit, before my crisis, my spiritual life was another aspect I tended to take for granted.

But, as I referred to in the last chapter, my best friend Ed was such a help at this time. Every Sunday he opened the pages of the Word and presented nuggets of truth that I had never seen before. Without his even realizing it, God was using Ed to gently bring me back to a place of genuine excitement about His Word.

THE MENTALITY OF A HEALTHY IDENTITY

In the Proverbs there is a well-known verse: "For as he thinks within himself, so he is."[1] I have begun thinking more and more about the wisdom in spreading out the areas in which I gain my identity. This mental process is where it must begin for all of us. It is not a matter of externals as much as it is internals. When I develop the thought patterns of a person with a healthy identity, I will see those lead to the appropriate actions.

Much of my thinking has turned to the language of the investor and the stockbroker. When they make themselves available to invest your money, they usually seek to ascertain if you are a conservative investor (small risk, small return), or a bit more of a gambler (greater risk, greater chance of return).

I am very much of the conservative species, and I have discovered that the way to avoid the big hits that can come from a major risk is not only to invest in conservative avenues, but also to *diversify*. By diversifying your portfolio, you have a broad financial base. Thus, if anything happens to any one of your investments, you are invested broadly enough to cover the loss and continue to make a little money (emphasis on *little*).

Diversifying is not only good advice for financial investors, it is equally wise for all of us who wish to develop a healthy identity. When the storms of crisis and disappointment hit, and they most certainly will, the broader our base, the stronger we will be, and therefore better braced for the hit.

Take some time to reflect on the meaning of this chapter in your own life. It might be advantageous for you to write out the areas of interest in your life. Are you diversifying? What needs to be added or subtracted in your overall picture? What should you emphasize more and what less? Make this a chapter of practical significance by applying it personally.

CHAPTer 9

This
Is Why God
Gives Us
FRIENDS

The better part of one's life consists of his friendships.

—Abraham Lincoln

If I had to go through the deepest waters of my crisis all over again, I would do one thing very differently: I would reach out to my friends much earlier in the process.

In my particular circumstance, I found my catastrophe to be extremely *embarrassing*, so I felt restrained from letting anyone in on the details of my pain. I feared people would judge me, condemn me, and offer lectures on morals and values that would degrade me. Emotionally, I was in no position to handle that sort of treatment.

So, I lived a life of quiet desperation. No one outside my immediate family knew what was going on for several *months*. I discreetly canceled any existing speaking engagements, taking me out of the work-force, so life consisted of a daily drive to the post office to pick up my mail, followed by a trip to the bank to make another withdrawal so I could pay for the groceries at my next stop. I became pretty good at things that kept me from dealing directly with people in any meaningful way—things like avoiding eye contact, keeping conversations on a superficial level, changing the subject at a moment's notice, and generating a fake smile that came from absolute devastation.

May and June of 1993 were horrible. Spring was in full bloom in our beautiful northern California town, but I saw precious little of it. It really didn't matter that in the foothills of the Sierra the daffodils, the tulips, and the roses were smiling. I wasn't. I was hiding indoors, mostly in the darkness, terribly afraid that someone would discover my secret and expose me for the failure I was.

By July I was in pretty bad shape. I started feeling like a change in scenery might be a help, so I proposed to the kids that we'd take a few days and drive to southern California. "I've got some free passes to Knott's Berry Farm from when I spoke there, so what if we go there one day and hit the beach another day and generally just kick back?" I suggested. The gang didn't need their arms twisted. That part of the country has been a favorite of theirs for a long time, since we used to live there, and I also sensed they felt the same need for a change of pace in their precious lives.

I never took a trip to Orange County without letting my best friend down there know. So, the day before we left, I called my buddy, Joe Davis, to see if we could get together.

"Hey, Joe. It's Bill," I said, trying to generate an excitement that sounded genuine. He asked how I was doing. "I'm bringing the kids down for a little vacation," I replied, completely avoiding his question. "I was wondering if we could visit a little when we're in your area."

"Sure. That would be great," he said. "What works out best for you?" I could hear him reaching for his calendar.

"Actually, we'll be down there tomorrow evening," I answered, while thinking through the best strategy. "Could you swing by the motel we'll be staying at after dinner tomorrow? We can talk while the kids swim in the motel pool."

"That works perfectly for me," Joe replied. "I'll see you poolside at seven tomorrow evening. And Bill, I want you to know I'm really looking forward to seeing you again. It's been too long."

He hung up the phone. As I hung up mine, my stomach tightened into one giant knot. *What did I just get myself into?* I thought as I began to panic. *I've left myself two options: I can either tell Joe everything that's happened in the last few months, or I can attempt to bluff my way through the whole thing.*

I was uncomfortable with both choices. Unsure if I wanted to spill my guts, I also didn't know if I could stonewall one of my best friends. I had visions of him seeing right through my facade, which would only make the truth that much more painful to confront. There was little sleep to be found that night.

I was tormented with my dilemma for the entire eight hours we were on the road the next day. I wanted to tell *someone*, but I was so afraid of how the person would respond. The more I pondered, the more I realized that if there was anyone who would be a compassionate listener, it would be Joe.

I first met Joe Davis when we both were working at *Insight for Living*. I had been on the counseling staff there for a couple of years when the word starting spreading that a new vice president of finance had been hired. Such a person can easily become the company's "hatchet man," and even though I wasn't abusing any funds, I was still a little intimidated by a guy who wielded that much power.

So, imagine my surprise when I expected Attila the Hun and instead I got Wally Cleaver. Yes, Joe Davis became the older brother I never had. We quickly bonded and I came to covet his counsel more than any other man's. The son of a country preacher, he had a firm background in his faith. He made his reputation in the business world as a man of flawless integrity, yet he had survived his own share of life's catastrophes in personal, family, and business venues. He had a beautiful bride, Molly, who was a constant and loving support to our friendship.

Over the years, Joe had been so influential on many decisions, both big and small, in our family's life. He had helped me see the wisdom in launching my own full-time speaking career back in 1987. He was there when I needed to discuss the pros and cons of relocating from Los Angeles to Grass Valley the following year. He counseled me on car loans, home mortgages, and income tax issues, as well as to buy the best brand of motor oil and how to most helpfully talk to my Little Leaguer who was putting too much pressure on himself.

The more I thought about Joe, the more I realized this date by the pool was all in God's master plan. It was even perfect that we were going to be poolside. I knew it was unlikely that I could get through this story without breaking down and crying, so this way it would look like my face was wet from being splashed by some overzealous kids working on perfecting their cannonballs.

And so it was that on a warm Thursday night, July 8, 1993, casually reclining on turquoise-and-orange-padded lounge chairs by the pool at Howard Johnson's Motor Lodge, in the shadow of the Magic Kingdom on

Harbor Boulevard in Anaheim, California, I finally opened up to one of my best friends.

After the kids swam over to greet Joe, they kept themselves occupied with a variety of water games so Joe and I could talk relatively uninterrupted. I sensed the older ones knew what was up.

"Where's Rhonda?" Joe innocently inquired, craning his neck as he searched the entire pool area.

"Sit down, buddy," I invited. "I've got something I need to tell you."

He took his seat pretty quickly, sensing there was something wrong. I swallowed hard, took a deep breath, and began sharing what had transpired over the last few months. Just as I expected, I wasn't very far into the conversation before the tears began flowing freely. I was so glad I decided to do this by a hotel swimming pool—they even provided towels.

As I recall, Joe didn't do a lot of talking that night. Rather, he did exactly what I needed him to do: He simply listened as I talked about loneliness, failure, rejection, insecurity, low self-esteem, no money, no hope, and no future. Occasionally he reached over to put his hand on my shoulder. Wisely, he chose not to wax eloquent. "Bill, right now I think the most important thing I can tell you is that I'm here for you and I will support you in any way I can."

Right before the evening ended, Joe asked me, "Does Mike know about any of this?"

"No," I whispered.

Mike Scott was a mutual friend of ours. A hardworking business executive living in Omaha, Nebraska, Mike, his pretty wife, Marcia, and their three adorable girls, Allison, Beth, and Katie, were a solid Christian family. The Scotts had attended family conferences I had conducted over the years and a friendship blossomed through some one-on-one time Mike and I had stolen here and there.

One particularly memorable conversation with Mike occurred about six years ago, when men everywhere were just becoming introduced to "bonding." Mike and I were lamenting the fact that so much of this bonding was occurring over such activities as fishing and hunting and camping out.

"Do you do any of that stuff?" Mike asked.

"No, I don't," I sighed.

"Neither do I," Mike said. Then, as an afterthought, he threw in, "Do you play golf?"

"Yeah—now that's something I really enjoy doing."

"Me too," he said. We stopped talking for a minute while the mental wheels turned.

"How about if we get together and bond over a long weekend of golf?" Mike anxiously suggested.

"That sounds great!"

"Okay, let's each invite one other guy so we have a foursome and we'll meet this January down in Phoenix."

At that moment we gave birth to a tradition that is now in its seventh year. Mike invited his friend Ron Nelson and I invited my friend Joe Davis. We meet for three or four days every winter with the excuse of playing golf, but the truth is we've become like brothers helping each other through life's demands.

In honor of our roots, with our tongues firmly planted in our cheeks, we called the group the FA-HARI COMB Society (Fishing And Hunting And Roughing It, Camping Out, Male Bonding). We've been slaving away at some golf resort faithfully now every year. It's become an annual highlight of my life.

So, when Joe asked if Mike knew what was going on, it was a very logical question. We had all become very close, but because we were in different cities, it had been as easy to keep Mike from the truth as it had been Joe.

YOU DON'T HAVE TO BE ALONE

"I haven't told Mike for pretty much the same reason I didn't tell you," I explained to Joe by the pool. "I'm so humiliated by this whole thing, I just haven't had the guts to call him up and tell him."

Joe proceeded very cautiously at this point. "I can sure understand why you feel the way you do, even though you have no reason to feel that way." Then he added, "Would you be comfortable if I called and told him?"

I shrugged my shoulders, replying, "Sure, I guess that's okay."

"I think it would be good for him to know," was Joe's nondescript response. With that, we embraced, Joe said good-bye to the kids, and he drove off. That was about 10 P.M., Thursday night. Apparently he went straight home and placed a call to Mike in Omaha. This is a pretty safe guess, because at nine o'clock the next morning there was a knock on the door of my motel room.

It was Joe . . . with Mike.

Mike burst into the room, arms outspread, hugged me and said, "I got here as fast as I could."

"Mike—" was all that would come out of my mouth, as my eyes filled with tears instantaneously.

"A guy going through what you're going through shouldn't be alone at a time like this," he assessed. Mike quickly laid out his strategy for the day. "I don't want to get in the way of your kids' vacation, but I did want to spend some time with you. Have your kids been to Disneyland this trip?"

"No," I answered. I didn't want to tell him I was broke and the only reason we were even going to Knott's Berry Farm was because I had free passes.

"Well, here's what I'd like to propose," Mike said. "I'd like to buy each of your kids a ticket to Disneyland. Two of Joe's kids, Jenny and Jeff, have volunteered to keep an eye on them while they visit over there, so there's no need to worry about them. And then Joe and you and me could have all day to be together to do whatever we want."

It's hard to look back and discern what was the most meaningful gesture that was on the table at that time. I didn't know if it was five tickets to Disneyland, or the look of genuine love and concern in Mike's eyes, or the look of reassurance coming from Joe as his eyes were saying, "See, Bill, there are people who genuinely care about you. It's about time you were on the receiving end of all this."

Needless to say, the kids were thrilled with the unanticipated pleasure of going to Disneyland, so they left soon after with Jenny and Jeff, all seven of them laughing and joking like reunited school chums. Mike, Joe, and I headed into a concentrated time of allowing me to flush a million feelings from their hiding places deep inside me out in the open for one of the first times since my pain began.

We started in the tiny motel room, moved to poolside when we needed to stretch, relocated to the coffee shop when we got hungry, and walked all around Anaheim when we wanted to exercise a little. All the time they were listening and helping me process the stuff that was trapped in the tiny strands of my emotional web.

LESSONS ON FRIENDSHIP

I realized some very important results during that

trip to Anaheim. First, I experienced firsthand how helpful it was to be able to talk to someone about my pain. During this time I was seeing a counselor, but being with some friends was a different context. That trip caused me to understand why God gives us friends. We were never intended to bear life's burdens alone. Friends are there to share the good *and* the bad. In both they aid us. They can make the good even better and the bad less painful.

Secondly, I saw how needless my stress was in fretting over what my friends would think. After all, if they were really friends, they would be there for me. I know my friends would have corrected me on issues if that had been necessary, but this was not a development in my life that needed their chastening. It was written all over my face—I needed love, and that's what they gave me.

Men, especially, are afraid of committing to a friendship that involves depth. And, for that very reason, when a man faces disappointment square in the face, he feels completely, and totally *alone*. I am learning how my friendships broaden my basis for understanding what is going on in my life. Guys like Joe and Mike give me a perspective I would otherwise never observe.

In business, we would never enter a risky endeavor without getting the counsel of a few trusted associates. In the medical world, getting a second opinion has become almost a cliché. We counsel our kids to talk with us before they make any major decisions. Yet, in many a man's personal life, we operate solo. I did it, and boy, is it ever a dangerous setting.

When all the hype concerning "accountability groups" hit the scene a few years ago, many men made positive strides in this area. But I have discovered that even guys in accountability groups can play the masquerade game. The bottom line is, we let people in on exactly what we want to in our lives—no more, no less. Accountability isn't a cure-all, either. People who are accountable to other people still experience the same catastrophes, the same pain, and the same disappointments.

But close friends are still the way to go.

NEW DIRECTIONS

When I returned to Grass Valley after this trip, there were two guys who were on my team. As I look back, I am still overwhelmed at how much they did for me. Mike and Joe made certain that one of them talked with me on the phone *every day* that summer. I imagine they worried that I could be on the roof of my one-story house, ready to jump to my death twelve feet below.

Shortly after my trip south, the fourth member of FAHARI COMB got involved as well. Ron Nelson started calling frequently, just to check on me, chat about whatever, and let me know he was praying for me.

Coupled with their concern for my emotional state, these three guys shared my burden relating to unemployment. "We need to get you working again," was their unanimous vow of involvement.

My network of friends starting checking in from all over the country. A few months later, in November, Mike invited me to come to Omaha for a little visit. It was a wonderful chance to recharge my emotional battery with good friends. On the way back, I had also arranged to stop over in Denver to visit another set of longtime friends, Ken and Judy Gire.

Ken and I, like Joe and I, go back to the days we worked together at *Insight for Living*. Ken is one of the most gifted writers I've ever met. As a testament to that fact, when I left IFL to launch a career as a full-time speaker (which people scoffed at, saying I'd starve to death), Ken left IFL to become a full-time *writer*, which I view as an incredible accomplishment! That's how talented this guy is.

As Ken and I sat on the deck that extends from his lovely home up in the Rockies, the conversation moved through the circumstances of the past months, ultimately ending up with future work options.

"You've always been such a good writer," Ken encouraged. "I think you should get back into it!"

"But I don't have anything I really want to say at this point in my life," I confessed.

"What about ghostwriting?" he countered (thereby inspiring my later call to Robert Wolgemuth). "Publishers are always looking for people to write other people's stories. With your personality and ability to get along so well with people, you'd be great at it."

I had never thought of writing for other people. "Plus it's a way to work while you're at home with the kids," Ken continued. "You'll have to make some trips to interview the person you're working for, but beyond that, you can work right there in Grass Valley . . . it would be perfect for you."

For the first time in a long time, I started to feel the slightest flicker of *hope*. Ken's loving prodding was responsible for that glimmer. The night before I returned home, Ken and Judy took me out to a fancy restaurant to celebrate my future success! I was overwhelmed with their feelings of love and support. It was so reassuring to have friends who believed in me, even when I didn't believe in myself. To underscore his encouragement, the next week he sent me not one or two but *eleven* books on how to succeed at this newfound craft! With titles like, *The Art of Ghostwriting, How to Conduct an Interview, How to Write with a Collaborator*, and so on, I was once again overcome with the generosity of my friends.

Upon returning home, I called Mike and Joe and

Ron to share the excitement of my new vocational prospect. Down to the man, every one of them was genuinely thrilled for me. "I can just see you now, writing away on your computer, logging page after page of quality literature for all the world to read!" was Mike's statement of support.

It was at that point I realized a new inadequacy. "I don't have a computer!" I admitted. "All the books I've done in the past were written longhand with a Bic pen on yellow legal pads."

"Welcome to the nineties, Mr. Butterworth!" Mike replied, laughing out loud. Then he added, "You've got to have a computer."

"Yeah, that would be great."

The next day, Mike called back, saying, "Give Ron a call. He's got some information on a computer that he wants to tell you about."

I knew Ron was a big-time computer junkie, but I found Mike's request a little confusing. *Why would I want information on a computer at this point in my life? I can't afford it,* I said to myself.

Then Joe called. "Have you talked to Ron yet?" he asked.

"Uh, no, not yet."

"Well, do it!"

So I called Ron. "I was expecting your call," he began. "I found a great deal on a computer for you."

"You have?"

"Yeah. It's a laptop, which is what you really need. You can travel with it to your interviews with these people. It's really convenient—you'll absolutely love it!"

I sat in stunned silence. *What is going on here?* I thought frantically.

"Plus," Ron added, "I've got a line on a great laser printer and a color monitor you can use when you're at home. Just connect your laptop to the monitor and everything will be twice as big!"

Ron went on and on about all the software that was included in this great deal he had negotiated. *It really sounds fantastic,* I thought as Ron continued, *but aren't we putting the cart before the horse here?* Finally, Ron was through describing the total package. I swallowed hard and asked the dreaded question, every muscle in my body tightening.

"How much is all this gonna cost?"

Ron's reply floored me. "For you? *Zero!*"

After a moment of silence, I finally squeaked out, "I don't understand."

"What is it about *zero* that you don't understand?" he laughed.

Either all the FAHARI COMB guys were chipping in to do this or one of them was picking up the tab, but in some gracious configuration, they were buying me a computer, setting me up for my still-uncertain future as a writer.

"Oh, Ron," I managed to utter before I once again began weeping uncontrollably. I was so unaccustomed to feeling the love and warmth of friends. It was more than I could handle without making a puddle by the phone.

The next day, Federal Express delivered five or six boxes of friendship directly to my front door.

As God's timetable revealed itself, it was just about this time that I made contact with Robert Wolgemuth, who, as I mentioned back in Chapter 2, began putting in motion a new world of ghostwriting for me. In a short time I was back to work again, all because a few choice friends surrounded me with an unconditional love and support that could not be suppressed by any negative emotion I could surface. They loved me in spite of myself, and I just couldn't fight it.

Robert quickly became more than an agent. The more we talked, the more I felt drawn to his genuine concern for me as a person. To this day, we talk on the phone almost daily, which is a lot more than we need to cover business issues.

THE BEAT GOES ON

Part of the joy of friendship is its reciprocal nature. More than ever I have appreciated the opportunities to be a listening ear to Mike or Joe or Ron or Ken or Robert or Gary or Ed or whoever. When I regained my emotional equilibrium, I was able to return the favors that had been afforded to me. Granted, none of these guys has gone through a similar circumstance in his marriage, but all of them have had their share of pain. The least I can do is be there for them, as they were there for me.

But, lest I be misunderstood, friendship is not really about keeping score. If I'm not careful I can fall into this trap. I don't "owe" these guys big-time for their friendship. I have always had such a difficult time accepting love unconditionally that I have to keep reminding myself of that truth. And my experience tells me there are lots of others out there who fall into the same "payback" category.

Beyond the reciprocal nature of these close friends, I have also begun to learn how God will use me to help others who may not come from my small circle of intimates. The more I feel comfortable sharing the lessons I am learning as a result of my crisis, the more I meet people in common concern.

George was a casual acquaintance at best. Our paths had crossed occasionally over the last ten years, but we never spent any time together beyond an occasional lunch when I was in his neck of the woods on the central California coast.

A few months ago I was asked to speak at a fundraising banquet for a parachurch ministry in the Bay area. The director of the organization wanted a message underscoring the importance of family. But he added, "There will be a lot of people at this banquet who are single parents, so, if you are comfortable doing so, let them know a little about your recent months and I know they'll come away encouraged by your words."

Well, it was amazing to me. For all of the remarks I made in a thirty-five-minute speech, it was the two minutes that I talked about my single-parent status that caused people to line up after the banquet to speak with me. The more I travel, the more I see throngs of people with this experience in life, and my friend was correct, they do need encouragement.

In the middle of this line was George. "You're not gonna believe this, Bill, but I'm going through the same thing you've just been through," he whispered.

That conversation began a series of conversations that continued by phone for the next few weeks. Sure enough, George was experiencing a nearly identical scenario to mine. The major difference was time. I was about nine months ahead of him in the process. As I heard him on the other end of the phone, it was easy to recall the feelings and emotions of nine months previous, because they were exactly alike.

However, with some time on my side, I was able to distinguish healthy thoughts from unhealthy thoughts, which was something I was unable to do back then. George was still in the fog I had come through.

It was gratifying to be able to help George think through some issues. Were it not for a good sounding board, George could have made some serious mistakes. I thought back to all the conversations I had with Mike and Joe. If not for their loving counsel and firm admonitions, I could have ended up in far worse shape. To be used in George's life the way Mike and Joe were used in mine was a true honor. It was more than I ever imagined.

One other friend who has been conspicuous by his absence in this chapter is Ed Neuenschwander. I talked about Ed in great detail in Chapter 7, so I felt that the story of Mike and Joe was especially relevant to this chapter. But one thing that needs to be said about Ed is that he was *local*. I am so very close to Ed today because we live in the same town. As much as the others have contributed to me in the last few years, they themselves would be the first to admit that there are obvious limitations because I live in northern California, Joe lives in southern California, Mike lives in Nebraska, Ron lives in Washington, and Gary lives in Arizona.

So I am learning the importance of a friend right where I live. It's been so encouraging to be able to call up Ed and meet him at our local coffee shop for a hot cup or at our favorite Chinese restaurant for an inexpensive lunch—to be able to look him in the eye and rejoice about some good news or weep together when some new pain rears its ugly head. He's been there for me dozens of times, and I am truly grateful.

WHAT GOES AROUND COMES AROUND

Back in the beginning of the book I related our family's encounter with a possible hurricane when we were still living in south Florida (remember, "Evacuate immediately, go inland, and north!"). That evacuation provided us with a fascinating exercise: Take everything you ever want to see again and put it in your car, knowing that what you leave behind you may never see again. I often tell this story when I speak. When I get to the part where we have to make our first choice of what to take with us in the car, I always stop and ask the audience to yell out what they think our first choice would be.

Almost always they call out "photo albums" or "pictures." Every once in a while I hear "makeup," but photos still win hands down. I think that's because photos are irreplaceable. How could you ever replace all those pictures?

A friend of mine knows a family who lived out this exact scenario. Several months ago, he shared their story with me. It's really quite a remarkable story about family, photos, and friends.

While vacationing out of the country one summer, this family's house caught fire and burned completely to the ground. Nothing was recovered . . . nothing.

When the family was alerted, they took the first flight back to their hometown. Maybe there was a little denial going on. Perhaps they hoped that there was a horrible mix-up and it wasn't their house that was destroyed. Slowly driving into their neighborhood, they turned left down their street, and there was no escaping the reality. Their lovely house and all that was in it were gone forever.

Every individual in the family had to go through the grieving process of all that was lost in that life-changing blaze. As time went on, most of the family members seemed to come to the place of acceptance concerning what had occurred. Eventually everyone seemed at peace, except Laura, the wife and mom in this home.

The source of her pain was the loss of all the family photographs. The unthinkable had transpired in her life. Those irreplaceable pictures were gone, burned beyond recovery. Laura went into a depression.

But one day she was on the phone from the tiny rented apartment they were living in during the interim period. "I'm just devastated by the loss of our photo albums," she told her friend Angela.

"I know your pain must be unbearable," Angela said, "everything gone and no way to get those precious pictures back. I wish there was something I could do."

In the moment of silence that followed, Angela suddenly realized there *was* something she could do!

"Laura, I just remembered . . . you sent me a bunch of pictures last fall. I think they were from your summer vacation to Florida."

"That's right!" Laura responded with more energy than she had experienced in over two months.

"I'd be delighted to send back the pictures you sent us."

"Angela, this is wonderful," Laura interrupted. "You don't realize it, but you've just given me a terrific idea!"

"What did I say?"

"Well, you just made me realize that I have *always* gone to get our photos developed at a place here in town that gives double prints. And I have *always* sent the doubles to good friends like you. So, all I need to do is let my friends know of the catastrophe, and I imagine I could recover a large amount of the pictures!"

Angela was thrilled to hear Laura's bubbly personality surfacing. And of course, she immediately mailed the photographs back to Laura.

This story has such a happy ending. After making contact with all her friends, Laura received a copy of virtually *every photo* that had perished in the fire.

Selflessly, she had always given of herself to her friends, and now they had the incredible opportunity to give something very special back to her.

This is why God gives us friends.

CHAPTer 10

The Wisdom in Calling the **PLUMBER**

How many counselors does it take to change a lightbulb? Only one, but the lightbulb has to really want to change.

I've never been a tool guy. I don't work well with my hands. I've only recently learned the names of the tools, so that when someone is helping me fix something, I know what tool to hand him or her.

So when I strolled into the laundry room last month and instead of hearing *clomp, clomp* I heard *squish, squish*, I knew I was in deep water. Literally and figuratively.

The water heater had expired. It went to waterheater heaven and at the same time, lost its ability to hold water. So, for who knows how long, our water heater had traveled the path of a slow death. And as it slowly died, it routinely dripped water from its base onto the wood floor of the laundry room.

Since it died a slow, painful death rather than a quick and painless one, the floor had been absorbing moisture for quite a long time. Now it was completely soaked. I didn't even want to think about what was going on with the subflooring. By the time I was feeling the squish of moisture up through my shoes and into my socks, I knew it was time to do something to remedy the situation.

Yet I didn't know what to do. This water heater and I weren't even on a first-name basis. I had always referred to it as "the large, white tank that lives next to the washing machine." We had never been formally introduced, so I felt understandably awkward about entering the innards of a piece of equipment I had only a casual acquaintance with.

Luckily, my dad was visiting us at the time. He was a real tool guy, and I had always thought he could fix anything. He took a look at it and asked for a wrench and a screwdriver. Within ten minutes he had performed an amputation that yielded a piece of pipe, which needed replacement. "Let's go to the hardware store," he said. "They'll have a piece to match this one, and we'll be all set."

After driving around for a while, we found a hardware store. I was amazed at the products this store carried. Granted, I didn't know what any of them were, but I truly was amazed at what I saw. Dad found the part he needed, we bought it, and we were back in the laundry room thirty minutes later, in surgery.

Once the part was back on our water heater, we turned the main water valve back on. The result was less than encouraging. With water spraying everywhere, including all over both of us, my only thought was, *Who looks like Abbott and who looks like Costello?*

One of us eventually got to the main valve and turned it back off. Dad looked particularly forlorn, as he was not used to being bested by a piece of metal. I, on the other hand, had a lifetime of memories of strikingly similar situations. It was no big deal to me, just another day of metal over man.

"I'm gonna have to call the plumber," I mumbled. Dad winced at the use of the dreaded P-word.

"Do you have any idea what a guy like that will charge you for a job like this?" Dad moaned.

"What else can I do, Dad? We can't fix it. It's out of our league. We gotta get some help."

As I dialed the plumber's number, my dad's eyes narrowed, his jaw tightened, and his hopes fell. We were completely snookered by this strange white tank that lives by my washer. Calling the plumber raised the handyman's white flag. Dad's only consolation was that he was on the West Coast, not home in Pennsylvania, where he would be easily identified as the one with the plumber's truck parked outside his town house. Perhaps he could live this down. He certainly wouldn't volunteer any of this information to his friends when they inquired about his visit.

The plumber came over and conducted the post-mortem. Yes, the water heater was dead. It was not something to be surprised at, however. Based on his calculations, it had lived a good long life—maybe as many as a hundred water-heater years. But it was time for the removal of the body and for the entrance of its replacement. I think I saw a tear in the corner of Dad's eye as the plumber solemnly removed our friend from his post next to the washer. He carried it quietly to his truck, where he then threw it ingloriously onto a pile of rubbish headed for the metal recycler.

The plumber returned and within a short time (well, not too short of a time—after all, they charge by the hour, not by the job) he had replaced Old Faithful with its new comrade. This model was sleeker, more energy efficient, and a steal of a deal at a price that Dad reminded me would have bought a small car in his day.

"This is a small price to pay," I reminded Dad. "Think what it would cost to water-vacuum the entire house if we didn't get a professional in here to replace this thing. It was out of our league, we had to get help."

The tale of the plumber has been a good reminder of an important principle: When you're in a mess beyond your skills and knowledge, you'd better call in a professional to help you.

This took on a whole new meaning for me when I came to a place in my life where I needed the help of a professionally trained counselor. Through his loving direction, I was able to make some sense out of circumstances that were totally senseless to my untrained eye. A counselor can be one of God's finest gifts when dealing with life's disappointments. Many people have come to agree.

THE SNAKES OF SUICIDE

Andy and Bernadette Jenkins know the value of the plumber. Their lives went through a "neck-deep in water" time period that just about did them in. Were it not for the wise counsel of a trusted therapist, this story would have quite a different ending.

Andy was brought up in a strict Christian home, the son of a minister. From his earliest days, Andy was taught to walk with the Lord and to seek His direction for his life. Following what he believed to be God's will, Andy enrolled in the business program at the University of Arizona. Four years later, he graduated with honors and took a position in a major accounting firm. The job required that he move to New York City, but Andy approached it as an adventure.

Once he was set up in an apartment in northern New Jersey, Andy started looking for a church home. It wasn't long before he found just the right place for his spiritual growth. And, as is often the case, about three Sundays after settling in with this warm and friendly congregation, he met Bernadette.

"Bernadette Wilson was easy to spot," Andy recalls. "She sang in the choir—second row, fourth from the right." The long-flowing purple choir robes disguised her small, trim frame, but nothing hid her gorgeous smile and her beautiful red hair.

After eight months of steady dating, Andy and Bernadette became engaged. They were married three months later, right there in the sanctuary where they met. Their newlywed days were happy ones, Bernadette joyously setting up house for the two of them and Andy climbing the corporate ladder at his firm.

The years went by and the Jenkins had two children, a son, Andy, Jr., and a daughter, Missy. By then Andy was a fixture at his office, highly respected, well in demand, and handsomely compensated.

About three weeks after Andy turned thirty-nine, life started taking some strange twists. It all started when their senior pastor invited Andy out for lunch on a Thursday afternoon.

"Andy, I've got a proposition for you," Pastor Morrison began. "Don't give me an answer right away, but rather, take some time, talk it over with Bernadette, and get back to me when it's convenient."

"Okay," Andy replied. "Exactly what is your proposition?"

Pastor Morrison suddenly beamed from ear to ear.

"We had an elder-board meeting last night." He paused for effect. "And they have given me the go-ahead to hire a new member for our church staff." He paused again, then leaned over the table. "We want to hire an executive pastor and we want that position to be filled by you!"

He leaned back, obviously proud of his offer. He let it just sink in for a few minutes. "It's a good deal, Andy. Trust me."

Andy went home that evening and told Bernadette. He hadn't a clue how she would respond to this offer, so he was somewhat surprised when she showed immediate excitement.

"I think we should do it," she said. "It is a wonderful opportunity for you to use your gifts in a way that has a direct impact on the lives of people."

Interestingly enough, Andy was thinking the same way. For some time he had been silently praying that the Lord would direct him to a ministry opportunity where his gifts could be used.

So Andy accepted the position and ninety days later he was officially a member of the pastoral staff of this growing community church.

"The transition was tougher than I anticipated," Andy now recalls. "The difference between the corporate world and a church staff was like night and day. I felt a little bit like the hatchet man for a while, but eventually I settled into my position."

It seemed like Andy had just relaxed a little at the church when the next issue arose. "Actually, I had been on staff at the church a full eighteen months, but it still seemed like a short period," he remembered. "I got a phone call from a man who was the president of a large para-church ministry. His name and the ministry's name were immediately recognizable to me. To make a long story short, he was calling to offer me a job—an important job—the vice presidency in his worldwide organization.

"I was flattered. Bernadette and I were flown to their headquarters to check out the possibilities. Frankly, it was all like a dream. This guy really wanted me, and therefore he was promising me things that I should have realized could have never come to fruition.

"The big drawback was that the job was in Colorado. It's a beautiful state, but it was going to be a major move for our family. Bernadette assured me that she and the kids would adjust. I guess she could see in my eyes that I really wanted this position. So, I accepted it and we moved."

The move was hard for the kids. They were of the age where they had established friends in New Jersey and the thought of leaving them caused some pretty major heartbreak. But Andy jumped headfirst into his new responsibilities. He made lots of friends and fulfilled his job assignments with his usual thoroughness.

"I was only in this job for three months when I knew I had made a big mistake," Andy admitted. "I guess I was fairly naive in thinking that all my boss promised me would actually happen. When I saw that some of it would *never* happen, I got real angry. I felt I had been deceived, as if the guy had told me exactly what I wanted to hear, whatever it would take to get me to accept the position. I had moved my family across the country and I was completely miserable in my job."

Andy took matters into his own hands. He began placing calls to some of his old buddies back in New York. One of his friends had launched off and created a firm of his own. "Want a job, Andy? It's here waiting for you!"

So that's how Andy moved his wife and kids back to northern New Jersey in less than a year from when they had moved away!

"I was angry and bitter," he confessed. "I didn't have a lot of love for my fellow Christians at this particular time in my life."

It was soon after that the story even intensified. "I'll never forget it. I walked into my office one Monday morning and my friend, my boss, the guy who had invited me back here, strolled into my office and calmly said, 'Andy, we're in some tough financial waters. We've decided to make some cutbacks in personnel, and unfortunately, that includes you. We'll do our best with a severance package, but it won't be much.'"

Andy went home and shared the shocking news with Bernadette. They both broke down and cried uncontrollably in each other's arms.

The next few months were pure torture for Andy. "I was to discover the dark side of life. The side that includes welfare lines, employment bulletin boards, and endless job interviews with no follow-up appointments."

Almost a year went by before Andy was able to secure another job. "Ironically it was with another group of guys who had broken off from the original firm I worked with. Their business was booming, so I finally got to a place where I was useful again."

Andy thought that working again would be the cure-all to his nagging emotional worries. But he was wrong.

"I entered the most horrible time of my life," he now admits. "I became incredibly depressed—more and more each day. I finally reached the point where I was seriously considering suicide.

"I'd wake up every morning, go downstairs, and have breakfast with Bernadette, Andy, Jr., and Missy. I'd look into their loving faces, hear their innocent chatter, and feel this overwhelming voice inside of me saying, 'Your family is better off with you dead than they are with you alive!'

"I had investigated my life-insurance situation and knew it was true. I was worth more dead than alive.

"It was this total feeling of depression that led me to seek out the help of a counselor. I had always been wary of professional help. They were 'shrinks' just out to steal your money and walk you through a lot of useless childhood memories that leave you no better off than when you started.

"But I've completely changed my tune," Andy admitted. "My therapist is a strong Christian, a wise counselor, and a good friend."

"He was the one who helped me put together the fragments of my life. It was at my first session with him that I realized after all those years of stability, I had just come through four job changes in four years! No wonder I was so rattled inside.

"'Andy, this is what I hear you saying,' he said to me after a few weeks. 'It's like you have just been fighting for your life against a giant cobra. Except in your case, it wasn't one cobra, it was four.

"'After a battle of that intensity and especially of that duration, it is quite common to have an adrenaline letdown accompanied by an emotional letdown.

"'What I'm saying, Andy, is that it is no wonder that you're suicidal! You are having a major downer after killing all those snakes!'"

Andy looks back to that session as a real turning point in his emotional growth. "It may not sound like a big deal to you, but it opened a door for me," he asserted. "Up to that point I had never allowed myself to *feel* the tremendous pressure I was carrying."

"That's when I started feeling it and working through all that was necessary to regain a position of strong mental health. Before I went to counseling, I had the mistaken notion that life was a straight line graph, moving on an upward slope the entire way. After a few months in therapy, I realized that life has its ups and downs. I am very confident that I am back on track today and I know it would never have happened were it not for my counselor. I am eternally grateful for this man's impact in my life."

Andy's lesson was a personal one just for him. It may be that someone else doesn't need a counselor to learn that lesson, but perhaps there is another lesson that can come only through a counselor.

WHO'S RESPONSIBLE FOR THIS MESS?

In the first chapter I told you about my friends, Brent and Elizabeth, who were having to endure the pain of their rebellious daughter, Michelle, a wayward sixteen-year-old.

"It was the hope that we could get Michelle in for some counseling that first led us to our wonderful therapist," Brent admitted. "Initially we had no intention of counseling for Elizabeth and me.

"We talked Michelle into visiting Dr. Morgan with us. She said she would go one time and she made no promises beyond that. We figured once was better than nothing at all, so we set up the appointment.

"Michelle vented a lot of anger at that session," Brent recalls. "Elizabeth and I were barely able to say a single word. Dr. Morgan mostly listened as well, only occasionally guiding Michelle by asking a leading question.

"Unfortunately, Michelle was true to her word. 'I went once—that's it,' she announced in the car on the way home. Elizabeth and I were crestfallen. We so wanted her to pull out of this rebellion and return to being the sweet little girl we had known.

"When I called Dr. Morgan to cancel the next appointment, he understood our disappointment in Michelle's unwillingness to attend. 'But I'd still like to see you and Elizabeth,' he said.

"What happened was the beginning of a six-month journey of the soul. We were overcome with feelings of guilt and failure. Dr. Morgan picked up on it almost immediately and we began dealing with some of the key issues that led to our distress.

"The bottom line was that we both felt personally responsible for Michelle's rebellion. We beat ourselves up with a list of circumstances that we felt could've made a difference in the way Michelle turned out. It was typical stuff—if we had given her more attention, if we would have been more faithful attending church, if we had been stricter here, more lenient there—the whole ball of wax.

"Dr. Morgan helped us see that Michelle was old enough to be responsible for her own actions. We could second-guess till we were blue in the face, and it wouldn't make any difference in the current circumstance. It sounds very basic, but it was the exact message that we needed to hear at that time in our lives. It was like a burden of lead weight was removed from our backs. We felt a degree of relief that we hadn't felt in a long time."

Brent added, "I'd be kidding if I said counseling took *all* the pain away, but it helped in a tremendous way. And to think we would have never thought of going to see a counselor for ourselves."

SNEAKING SOME SESSIONS

My journey toward counseling is almost funny now as I look back on it. I had to come face-to-face with a large amount of hypocrisy on my own part to even get in the door to see a counselor. After all, I had *been* a counselor for over six years, yet I still held the foolish notion that I was above needing professional help.

Ultimately I reached the end of my rope. I knew my problem was beyond the help of a good friend, a mentor, or even a pastor. I needed someone who could help me sort out an avalanche of new emotions, all of them resulting in extreme pain.

One of my favorite speaking engagements before I got off the circuit was at the Mount Hermon Christian Conference Center, just outside Santa Cruz, California. I have always found the majesty of the coastal redwoods to be a lift to my spirits. Coupled with the fact that I had some of my finest friends on the staff down there, it was always a highlight on my speaking calendar.

My closest friends at Mount Hermon are Ken and Marilyn Harrower. For years they have invited me to speak at their summer family camps, which we attended with all five kids in tow. To this day the kids have some of their best growing-up memories at Mount Hermon. The Harrowers have also had me address couples' conferences and their wonderful Thanksgiving Conference as well.

It was at a Labor Day conference that I asked Ken and Marilyn if they would like to take a little walk around the great outdoors. Even now, I don't know for sure if they could sense the inner pain I was feeling, but if they did, they waited respectfully for me to bring it up rather than rudely probing.

During our walk through the redwoods, I finally got up the courage to ask for their help in getting me to a counselor. Well, I *kinda* got up the courage. I don't know how many times I have had others use this scam on me in the past, but I turned right around and used it on the Harrowers.

"I've got this friend up in Grass Valley who really needs some help," I began my tall tale of deception.

"A friend of yours?" Ken asked. He raised his eyebrows in such a way that leads me now to believe the masquerade was over before it began.

"Yeah, a real close friend," I continued.

"What kind of help does he need?" Marilyn asked.

"Basically, his life is falling apart," I replied. "His marriage is on extremely shaky ground right now, and it's really affected his personal life. He's going through a time of real insecurity and rejection."

"This sounds serious. . . . I'll get you a referral from my office before you leave this weekend," Ken offered. He put his arm around me and added, "No wonder you're so concerned about him."

I choked back the tears and finished our walk.

Ken was true to his word and I left the conference with the names of three counselors in the area who could help me. As I looked at their names and addresses, the choice was a simple one—a no-brainer. The criterion was far from scientific, or in any way based on ability to offer help . . . I chose the guy who worked the greatest distance from where I lived. Miles were meaningful to me.

I don't want anyone to know I'm seeing a counselor, I muttered to myself. *If I have to be mentally ill, I choose to be anonymously mentally ill.* And with that brave pronouncement, I began my saga with my counselor, Dan.

SO, WHAT'S ON YOUR MIND?

Sitting in the waiting room at a counseling clinic must feel a lot like standing in a police lineup when you know you are guilty. I nervously went up to the receptionist's window, where I was forced to say my name aloud. No one waiting even bothered to look up, but I was mortified. I felt like saying, "Just hand me the sign to wear that says, 'Hi, I'm Bill Butterworth. I am a very sick person, so you'll want to stay away from me.'"

Instead of a sign, the receptionist handed me a clipboard with an "Intake Questionnaire" to be filled out. I sat down in the sterile, all-white waiting room and felt my courage grow as I jotted down the intimate areas of my life—social security number, driver's license number, and my health insurance carrier.

But the last question squashed all intentions of bravery. "Why are you here?" was the query at the bottom of the page, with five or six lines of blank space provided. I nervously looked up at the others in the waiting room. *They could care less about me,* I realized. *They probably feel like I do: They just want to hide.*

I recall scribbling something incredibly unrevealing. "I am here to discuss some personal growth issues." *That isn't exactly a lie,* I rationalized. *Plus, if I put, "My life is in the toilet," the counselor might institutionalize me right on the spot.*

I turned in the clipboard and bit my nails to the

quick. It was fascinating to me how everyone waiting seemed incredibly gifted at avoiding all eye contact with each other.

Once I was ushered into Dan's office, I chose to sit on the plain, brown couch. I sat on one end, then took a tweed throw pillow from the couch and clutched it to my breast. This was to become my standard operating procedure throughout all my counseling sessions. One doesn't need to be an expert in nonverbal communication to interpret the message of insecurity I was showing my counselor.

"So, what's on your mind?" Dan began.

His first words threw me. My mind raced. Inside my head, I was screaming, *What? No small talk? No easing into this? What are you trying to do, cripple me mentally for life?* I felt like I was living out a seventies Woody Allen movie.

"What's on my mind?" I repeated, in a vain attempt to stall for some time. My mind wasn't cooperating.

"Yes, what brings you all the way down here from Grass Valley to see me? If I'm not mistaken, that's almost an hour's drive each way. Something must be troubling you. Can I be of help?"

This was the moment. I knew if I didn't shoot straight with him, I'd end up paying a lot of money for nothing. I needed him to pass just one simple test.

"Do you know who I am?" I asked. I knew I was far

from a household name, but there were a lot of people who knew of my speaking and writing.

"Uh, no, all I know about you is what you wrote on your Intake Form—which wasn't a whole lot." He stared down at the form and gently shook his head. He seemed a little baffled by my question.

I was absolutely anonymous. Feeling a blanket of protection through my unknown identity, I opened up and over the next few months told Dan just about every hurt I ever felt in life.

I honestly believe that I learned things in counseling that I wouldn't have learned through any other means. To think that I ruthlessly held on to the prehistoric notion that counseling was only for psychos and the hopelessly neurotic. I am so thankful for what counseling helped me do.

I learned to take responsibility for what was mine and to not take responsibility for what was not mine. A lot of what I was feeling was centered around the word *rejection*. My wife leaving me made me feel like I did for so much of my childhood, when I was the little fat kid who had no friends. Try as I might, I could only gain attention by performing humorous antics for my peers. And through these "performances," I gained the acceptance I so desperately craved. But by the time I was an adolescent, I was plagued with the realization that as the class clown, I was the life of every party, but

I still couldn't get a date on Saturday night . . . a serious form of rejection for a teenager.

This staggering fear of rejection led me to an overdependence on my marriage. In one particular session, when Dan asked me what I would do if my wife left, I came unglued. It was the ultimate rejection, I concluded, complete with all of its devastating pain.

This led to the realization that I believed I was a complete zero apart from my family. Since I had such little respect for myself, I would desire the security of my family in an almost-desperate way. And it was through this desperation that Rhonda felt smothered. I was trying to do the right thing, but it was having the opposite effect. As Dan said to me, "Bill, you're sucking the life out of her." Sure, she was making her own decisions, but there was a context to be considered.

So who am I? The identity issues that we discussed in Chapter 8 came into focus at this point in my journey. Discovering the many facets of my identity was another process that my counselor strongly encouraged.

Of course, there was a lot of anger inside me at this point as well. I was angry at this horrible situation in my life, but in reality, I was angry at myself for being so paralyzed by the situation. I was unhappy in who I was and that unhappiness, anger, and rejection were all intertwined into one large knot, most often found either in the pit of my stomach or square in the middle of my head.

I had to learn to deal with my faults in the breakdown of my marriage. It was easy to blame it all on someone else; easy, but not accurate. It was oversimplistic to say that my marriage ended for one reason. Granted, I did not file for divorce, but I had to own up to what I did do to contribute to its demise.

That wasn't easy for me to do, just as it isn't easy for me to write about it now. I have a history of looking for the easy way, as most of us do. I'm thankful my counselor guided me through the more difficult pathway and together we navigated it with an incredible amount of success.

My heart goes out to the one who has dealt with life's bitter disappointments and is still attempting to make sense of them while all alone. I hope you find encouragement in my story. Perhaps you can use it as a way to "give yourself permission" to reach out and take that first step toward some help.

People still debate about the need for and effectiveness of counselors today. If you decide to visit a counselor, listing some expectations will help you choose one who is appropriate to your needs. For example, in my case, it was essential to me that my counselor be a Christian. I wanted to be assured that we held the same basic value structure so that I would never be in a situation where I was being asked to do something that violated my moral base. I do have friends who have found wonderful help through non-Christian counselors, though I think that is a very risky endeavor. I also have friends who have had more extensive expectations in terms of their counselors' qualifications. They have needed the reassurance of not just shared faith but a clear understanding of their counselors' techniques and ways of integrating theology and psychology.

I understand that choosing a counselor is a very personal thing. All I am asking is that you don't let anything get in your way of that pursuit. I feel that your pastor is always a good place to begin in looking for a referral. Of course, if you are going "undercover," like I did, you'll need to polish up your "I've got a friend who needs help" story. Maybe you can be a little braver than I was.

Whatever it takes, make me a promise, okay? If you're feeling life's disappointments to the degree that there is a *squish, squish* sound coming from your feet as you walk life's path . . . promise me you'll call a plumber.

CHAPTer 11

Watch
GOD WORK

*God whispers in our pleasures,
but shouts in our pain.*
—*C. S. Lewis*

Did your life turn out the way you planned?"
Many characters from the pages of Scripture would be well qualified to answer that question. I'm not sure David ever planned on meeting Goliath. Sarah was more surprised than anyone when she discovered she was pregnant at ninety years of age. Abraham never planned on offering his son Isaac as a sacrifice. Joseph's imprisonment wasn't in his life plan.

But along with all these other people, I wonder how Moses would answer that question, if I could somehow ask him.

"Did life turn out the way I planned? No, life had some surprises that caught me off guard," would be my guess at his honest response.

"What turned out differently?" would be a legitimate follow-up question.

"Well, for one thing, when we left Egypt and headed east, I never expected to run smack into the Red Sea!"

MISERY

Moses is a man who knew disappointment first-hand. For four hundred years, the nation of Israel lived in humiliating slavery at the hands of the Egyptians. Led by their Pharaoh, they reduced God's chosen people to mere work-units. They were deliberately and consistently robbed of their personhood by godless people who treated them the same way African-Americans were treated in the first one hundred years of the history of the United States.

Yet Jehovah had a plan for Moses. He was to be the leader of these people. He would be the one used to orchestrate the great exit out of slavery and into the promised land. We have tended to make the Bible's heroes bigger than life, and in doing so we miss a valuable lesson. I believe Moses was a human being very much like you and me. He shared the same fears and insecurities that plague us all. So it was both a splendid honor and awesomely intimidating to be chosen by Jehovah as the individual who should stand before Pharaoh to speak on behalf of an entire nation of people.

With his insecurity clearly showing, Moses told God that he was unable to speak with Pharaoh, so God instructed him to have his brother, Aaron, accompany him to his appointments with the Egyptian leader.

The book of Exodus records this marvelous account of the nation's move from slavery to freedom. In chapter five, Moses and Aaron get their first opportunity to speak to Pharaoh. Shaking in their sandals, they stood firm.

> And afterward Moses and Aaron came and said to Pharaoh, "Thus says the LORD, the God of Israel, 'Let My people go that they may celebrate a feast to Me in the wilderness.'" But Pharaoh said, "Who is the LORD that I should obey His voice to let Israel go? I do not know the LORD, and besides, I will not let Israel go." [1]

The Egyptians were polytheists. They had gods and goddesses for all sorts of things. If this were a modern-day story, they would have such choices as the god of the car and the goddess of the chair, and the god of the microwave and the goddess of the VCR. They were an equal opportunity employer of deities. Thus, the implication in Pharaoh's words are, "We have many, many gods and goddesses, while you have *only one*, this one you call Jehovah. Who is Jehovah that I should listen to Him? What is your one God compared to our hundreds of deities?"

This sort of banter continued. It certainly must have been a frustrating time for Moses. Here's a guy who is clearly being directed by God to do something, yet it doesn't get accomplished. Can you imagine Moses' disappointment? He probably started talking to himself. *Gee, all God asked of me was to go to Pharaoh and gain the release of the people. . . . I'm not doing very well with this task.*

But God's timing was different than Moses'.

Jehovah was a little more patient with Pharaoh—but only up to a point. Even the Lord Himself eventually grew weary of Pharaoh's unwillingness to release His people. Pharaoh was a stubborn cuss. So God decided to answer one of Pharaoh's key questions: "Who is Jehovah that I should obey Him?"

To use the terminology of a schoolteacher, God answered that question with ten audiovisual presentations. We know them as the Ten Plagues. There were frogs and blood and lice and flies and animal plagues and boils and hail and locusts and darkness and death. If you studied the customs and beliefs of the Egyptians, you would see that each and every one of the plagues was a direct slap in the face of one of their gods or goddesses and through those disasters the true God was able to get Pharaoh's attention!

MOVIN' OUT

Imagine the scene in Egypt by the time the tenth plague struck. Already ravaged by the other nine, morale was at an all-time low in the homes of the Egyptians. The final plague was especially painful since it required the death of the firstborn in every Egyptian household. Yet it's worth noting that this death would not visit the children of Israel, "that you may understand how the

LORD makes a distinction between Egypt and Israel."[2] God was watching out for His people.

Death touched every Egyptian home. "Pharaoh arose in the night, he and all his servants and all the Egyptians; and there was a great cry in Egypt, for there was no home where there was not someone dead."[3]

Remember the culture we're dealing with here. This is not the more quiet, reserved Western world. No, this is the Middle Eastern culture, which expresses grief with cries, screams, and wailing. The louder the cry, the closer the griever was to the deceased. There was a mother in every house who was hoarse from manifesting her grief in utter despair.

It was so bad, according to the text, it sounded like one large cry. Pharaoh, who probably hadn't had a good night's sleep since the whole plague incident hit, once again awakened to the moaning of his subjects. If he were an elected official, this would have made for an approval rating that would have floored his political handlers. Dealing with criticism and lack of sleep is a horrible combination.

So Pharaoh gave in. In the middle of a sleepless night he called for a hastily arranged meeting with Moses and Aaron Then he called for Moses and Aaron and said, "'Rise up, get out from among my people, both you and the sons of Israel; and go, worship the LORD, as you have said.'"[4]

Pharaoh was giving them an Old Testament version of "Get outta town!" It would be easy to imagine that Moses felt validated with this pronouncement. *We're finally moving away from this misery to a new home!* he must have thought. If he only could have known it was going to get worse before it got better.

Moses and Aaron didn't wait around. Can't you just see them, hustling into action, running from tent to tent, pulling back the flaps, and yelling inside, "Let's go! Everybody up! We're outta here! Move it!" The children of Israel, still half asleep, perhaps didn't even understand. They must have replied in a semi-dazed state, "Why do we have to wake up in the middle of the night? Don't we work long enough hours as it is? Why are you doing this to us?"

"It's the Exodus!" Moses replied, making a mental note about a good title if he ever decided to write this into book form.

A few verses later, it's recorded, "Now the sons of Israel journeyed from Rameses to Succoth, about six hundred thousand men on foot, aside from children."[5]

Six hundred thousand men! Add to that an equal number of women, and you have one million two hundred thousand adults! On top of this, Pharaoh had once remarked how quickly the Israelites multiplied. So if that meant that each family had four kids (which is a pretty conservative estimate coming from a guy with five of his own), you would have to add another two million four hundred thousand children. This is an absolutely staggering concept, because when you put all of this together, you have *three million six hundred thousand men, women, and children.*

That is such a phenomenal number that it goes beyond the comprehension of most of us. It is only the certified public accountants who read these figures that have any grasp of the mind-boggling implications. For example, if that number of people was marching out of Egypt fifty abreast, it would create a column *forty miles long.* That means if they walked at two-and-a-half miles an hour, it would take more than sixteen hours for the back of the line to pass the same point that the front row had passed earlier that day!

I'll spare you how many boxcars of food it would take to feed them, or how many times they could circle the earth if they were placed head to toe, or how deep into space they could stretch. Trust me, it was a lot of people.

I raise that issue to further underscore Moses' job. It was no small task to lead three million-plus people out of Egypt. It's easy to assume that he felt like he was doing exactly what God wanted him to be doing . . . and he was. And it's often exactly those circumstances that make us feel immune to disappointment and crisis. A common thought among us Christians is, *Certainly if we're following God's directions, He won't allow us to suffer hardship, pain, or disappointment.* Bad stuff is for bad people. Good people experience life to its fullest, along with a large measure of joy, right?

Wrong.

MIND-CHANGERS

The plot started to thicken after Pharaoh had a chance to enjoy a much-needed good night's sleep. Then, with a clear head, he began to realize all that he had let go by releasing the children of Israel. He had willingly freed his slaves! This didn't sit well with him and soon he had second thoughts:

> When the king of Egypt was told that the people had fled, Pharaoh and his servants had a change of heart toward the people, and they said, "What is this we have done, that we have let Israel go from serving us?" So he made his chariot ready and took his people with him; and he took six hundred select chariots, and all the other chariots of Egypt with officers over all of them.[6]

Pharaoh decided he wanted his servants back, so he ordered the army out to retrieve them. He forgot the pain Egypt endured before he released the Israelites. Evidently Pharaoh was a real "live in the moment" kind of guy. All he knew was that he was fresh out of slaves, "so let's go round 'em up."

And that's exactly what he did. He took some of the

best men from his highly trained army and launched off after Moses and that three million-plus gang of his.

Moses was in for his share of crisis and disappointment. In many respects, it is the classic illustration of an impossible situation. For, while this was going on behind them, the front lines of the Israelites ran square into the Red Sea. God had decided not to send the Israelites on the direct route, but rather the scenic route, featuring fabulous views of the water. They didn't need to face the Red Sea to get to the promised land, but God had other ideas. The people started yelling, "Break out the boats! We're up against the Red Sea!"

It didn't take long for someone to raise this issue with Moses. "Where are the boats, boss? You're in charge of this excursion. Surely you brought the right equipment. Did you delegate this to someone?"

"I'm afraid we didn't bring any boats," Moses answered, seeing the disappointment register on their faces.

Can you imagine what happened next? Think of it this way: Remember the game "Whisper Down the Lane" that we played when we were kids? Someone in the front row of the classroom would tell a secret to the child behind him, and that child would pass it back to the next kid, and so on, until it got to the rear of the classroom. At that point the child would share the message with the whole class and everyone would laugh about how distorted it had become in being passed from one to another.

So imagine playing "Whisper Down the Lane" with three million people!

"We're up against the Red Sea—no boats—pass it back," was the message. It must have suffered some serious distortion being subjected to that many people. I wonder how that message changed?

"We're up against the Pacific Ocean and unless it freezes over, we're all doomed!"

Meanwhile, at the rear of the three million people, a little tyke was rubbing his nose with one hand and pulling on his dad's robe with the other. "Look, Dad! Look behind us! It's a real-live army! They've got some cool swords and shields and chariots and all kindsa really neat stuff! It's so rad!"

The father looked back, ready to lecture his son about his overactive imagination, but he saw the boy was correct. "Pharaoh has come to take us back to slavery!" he screamed. "We must defend ourselves— break out the weapons!"

At this point a realist in the group shouted back, "We've been slaves for four hundred years. How many weapons did you collect during that time?"

The man hung his head. Besides the little knife he carved out of a spoon, he was completely defenseless. Once he regained his composure, he started a game of "Whisper Up the Lane." He leaned forward to say,

"We're up against Pharaoh's army and we have no weapons—pass it up."

And so bad news traveled both directions, most likely getting more and more distorted as it moved.

Since we're doing this much imagining with this story (you didn't think I was getting *all* of this from the text, did you?), can you imagine the poor person who got both sets of bad news at the same time? Some sad guy was right in the middle of three million people. He got both shoulders tapped simultaneously. He turned to hear one guy say, "No boats," then turned the other way to hear, "No weapons." This could be the only casualty of the Exodus—one poor soul who suffers cardiac arrest right there in the wilderness! "Too much stress," the doctor would say in his medical report.

Meanwhile Moses was square in the middle of this mess. He had led the people to an impossible situation. With wilderness on each side, he had an uncrossable body of water in front of him and an army behind him.

MURMURING

Believe me, the children of Israel didn't take this lightly. Moses received far from a vote of confidence at this point:

> And as Pharaoh drew near, the sons of Israel looked, and behold, the Egyptians were marching after them, and they became very frightened; so the sons of Israel

cried out to the LORD. Then they said to Moses, "Is it because there were no graves in Egypt that you have taken us away to die in the wilderness? Why have you dealt with us in this way, bringing us out of Egypt? Is this not the word that we spoke to you in Egypt, saying, 'Leave us alone that we may serve the Egyptians'? For it would have been better for us to serve the Egyptians than to die in the wilderness." [7]

Talk about an impossible situation! Red Sea in front, Egyptian army behind, and a bunch of whiners in between! Sound like your situation? It was the height of sarcasm on the part of the people. "Did we ask you to bring us here?" they taunted. Moses had every right to respond, "Yes. For four hundred years that's all you people have been saying, day in and day out!"

"Didn't we say 'Leave us here in Egypt'?"

Not!

"You've been murmuring to get out of there for years and now that you're out, you're still murmuring!" could have been Moses' honest reply. By the way, could you imagine the sound of three million people grumbling? Even a quiet mumble multiplied by three million makes for an interesting sound effect, to say the least!

This was Moses' moment to deal with crisis beyond his wildest imagination. If there was ever a time a man could have expressed disappointment with God, it was then. He could have joined right in that chorus of murmurs. He could have lifted his arm, shook his fist at God, and placed the blame square on Jehovah's shoulders.

Remember, Moses was a regular guy like you and me. And he was in a bind. He hadn't read the book, he hadn't seen the movie, he hadn't been on the Universal Studios tour. He didn't have a clue concerning how this would all turn out in the end. Contrary to most of our popular mental perceptions, I'd like to suggest that at this time in his life he didn't even look that much like Charlton Heston.

No, Charlton Heston is bigger than life. With those broad shoulders and rugged good looks, very few of us can identify. Let's recast the role of Moses in our mental movie, okay? Let's choose a smaller guy, less handsome, maybe even a little squirrely at times, so we can better relate.

How about Dustin Hoffman?

The point is, Moses was a person just like you and me. And there he was, face-to-face with a situation he never planned on. Yet in his response to the people we can see how he transcended his human tendency toward panic; instead, he had faith.

MOSES' MIND-SET

In Exodus 14:13–14, I believe we see one of the finest strategies for coping with life's catastrophes and disappointments ever uttered. It is profound in its simplicity. After hearing all this griping and complaining, Moses turned to the people and offered this sage counsel for people of all times:

> But Moses said to the people, "Do not fear! Stand by and see the salvation of the LORD which He will accomplish for you today; for the Egyptians whom you have seen today, you will never see them again forever. The LORD will fight for you while you keep silent."

Just the opposite of his people, Moses offered us one of the most brilliant applications of how God works through crisis. I offer his prescription to you. I've applied it numerous times in my life and I know how helpful it can be.

He tells us to do four things and in doing those things we can feel the burden of life's disappointments lighten. Here are the four applications:

1. Do not fear.

The language in Exodus is "do not fear" but the original word refers to a fear that comes from anxiety. "Don't worry, be happy" might be a modern sound bite that today's media would use.

Fear is a crippler. Philip Yancey wrote in his wonderful book, *Where Is God When It Hurts?*, of fear's power:

Dr. Paul Brand illustrates the varying effects of pain by relating his experience as a medical technician in London during World War II. There, injured men shipped over from the Continent told him phenomenal stories of courage. Some who had taken shrapnel or bits of grenade in their bodies disregarded the pain to rush out under heavy fire and rescue their buddies. The British soldiers' spirits were so high that few went down immediately with injuries. Often they continued fighting until it became physically impossible. Brand treated these men, some with amputated limbs, some with enormous ulcerations as a result of their wounds.

Strangely, these heroes lost all bravery when time for antibiotic shots rolled around. Penicillin, a new discovery then, was primitively manufactured in the huge vats of a London distiller. Impure and slightly noxious, the drug was too irritating for the veins to receive large doses, so small doses were injected every three hours. The injection stung like acid.

Brand recalls being on night duty when the nurse came in at two o'clock with the penicillin tray. Moments before she entered, the men would wake from sleeping. They would lie in bed, eyes wide open, some shuddering. As they heard her approach, some would emit rueful groans. Adult men—the same daring soldiers who had risked their lives on the battlefield—would sob uncontrollably as the nurse approached them with the needle.

None of these men would argue that the prick of a needle dripping penicillin, painful though it was, exceeded their suffering on the war front. But other factors—their surroundings and anticipations—made the experience of a single penicillin shot more horrifying than that life-and-death conflict.

Fear seems to be the single common denominator which can push a painful experience into the realm of the unbearable.[8]

What was the difference between the battlefield and the hospital room? *Fear*. These brave, strong, courageous men, who put their well-being aside to rescue their friends, became absolutely paralyzed by fear.

Fear drains you of emotional strength. When people are in a crisis or a period of deep disappointment, they need all the emotional strength they can muster. That is why fear is so damaging to a person's insides. It robs you of vital elements that can be used to fight off these bad feelings.

I am not advocating *denial* here. If you have fears, you must confront them and deal with them. Not to do so is denying their existence, and that won't make them go away. They will just choose another time to erupt, and usually it is not a good time.

The writer of Proverbs understood this issue of fear when he wrote: "Anxiety in the heart of a man weighs it down,/But a good word makes it glad."[9]

Don't add excess baggage to your situation by fear, anxiety, and worry. Deal with it and put it behind you.

2. Take your stand.

The next piece of advice Moses gave the people is the phrase that reads "stand by" in many versions of the Scripture. But if you have marginal notes like I do in my New American Standard Bible, you'll observe that a more literal rendering of this phase from the Hebrew is "take your stand."

I can just see Moses making this suggestion. While uttering these very words, he is digging his sandals into the sand by the Red Sea. I say this because it is still early enough in the story that he has no idea how God is going to miraculously deliver them. So in my mind's eye, I see him bracing himself by the shoreline.

In a way, what Moses said was, "I don't know how we're going to get out of this mess, but we need to be prepared for whatever comes our way. So, take your stand, brace yourself, prepare to be hit!"

Over the last fifteen years I've been very fortunate to be invited to speak at the pregame chapel services for the teams of the National Football League. And over the years, I've spoken to just about all the individual teams. This is one of my favorite passages to present to the players, because it feels so alive to me.

When we get to this part of the story, I usually explain "take your stand" this way: "This is a verse for all the offensive linemen in the room. It's as if it were the fourth quarter, and you've been hounded by the same defensive lineman the entire game. He's very good, and he's actually gotten by you on a couple of plays. Back in the huddle, your quarterback is begging you for a little more time and protection. You nod your head, but inside you know you're giving it everything you've got.

"So you opt for a different strategy. The huddle breaks, you go to your position on the line of scrimmage, and you look squarely into the eyes of the defender. 'Look!' you yell, 'you've been killing me the whole game. I know we're both exhausted. So I'm gonna rest on this next play—I'm not even gonna get set in my stance—I'm just gonna stand here for one play and catch my breath. Now, if you're any sort of gentleman, you'll stay over on your side of the line and rest with me. Okay?' And then you turn to your quarterback and signal him that it's all right to hike the ball.

"When he hikes the ball, just as you promised, you haven't even gotten down into your stance. You're standing up straight in a very casual posture. Your arms are folded across your chest, you take a moment to catch your breath as you hope to watch this play unfold without your participation."

At this point in the chapel service I usually ask the guys, "What do you call a lineman who lines up this way?" And, of course, the answer is, a *former* lineman.

"This guy will never play again. He is going to get creamed by the opponent. Why? Because he hasn't taken his stand! He needs to be down in his three-point, or four-point stance, prepared and ready to get hit."

It's that sort of preparation that I see in Moses' admonition. Just as we didn't know this crisis or disappointment was going to hit us, in the same way, we have no idea how it's all going to work out. Thus, it may mean that we need to fight our way out. So we had better brace ourselves for the hits of the enemy.

It's kinda like the Boy Scout motto for all us adults: Be prepared.

3. Watch God work.

"See the salvation of the Lord, which He will accomplish for you today." Now there is a command that leaves an unbeliever in the dust. As children of God, we have an amazing relationship with our Father. He knows what is going on in our lives, and He can come to our rescue with the perfect solution to an imperfect scenario.

I remember reading a textbook in seminary that spoke eloquently concerning this predicament in the lives of the children of Israel:

The question rises as to why God led His people to a place where they would be trapped between water and pursuing Egyptians. A slightly different route, really no longer in distance, would have missed the Bitter Lakes entirely. The answer is clear that there was a need for just this sort of experience by the Israelites at the beginning of their long weary march through the wilderness. They needed a strong impression of the greatness of Yahweh's power, for they had been long in the land of Egypt where false gods were worshipped. They had forgotten how great in power the true God really was. The demonstrations of power in the plagues had helped, but most of these had occurred, intentionally, only in the Egyptian area. Israelites certainly had heard of them, but hearsay is never as impressive as direct experience. The people needed to see for themselves God's power, and here they did. They saw most vividly what God could do in controlling and redirecting forces of nature, and then employ them in turn to overthrow the world-renowned, mighty Egyptian army. The memory would have fortified the Israelites for meeting days of trial that lay ahead during the forty years of wilderness travel.[10]

Israel had to learn lessons about God it would have never learned in any other way. Many of us who have seen life turn out differently than we planned have to make the same discovery. There was something in that business bankruptcy that would have never been realized if the trauma had not occurred. The marital breakdown taught someone the essential quality of faith in the Lord. A death ultimately drew someone closer to God. The cancer was something of necessity.

It is in these catastrophes that we can watch God work. In the case of the Red Sea, He did actually perform a miracle. Your situation may not require such a bold move, but if it does, do not fear, God is still parting Red Seas today. There is never a guarantee that requires Him to do so, but nevertheless, He does.

In the last few months God has brought so many people into my life who have experienced the healing that can only come from His hand. Story after story of how people have watched God work—some miraculous, others not. In many and varied ways, God has made sense of their tragedies and brought them back to healing and wholeness. It is a distinct advantage of being His child.

Remember, watching God work is one of the directions in this prescription. Don't misread this as an admonition to passivity. It is not an isolated sit-back-and-do-nothing type of suggestion. We are watching God work by exercising our faith in Him. We watch God work while we brace ourselves for whatever situation may come, doing our best to put our fears behind us. It is when these four pieces are put together that we see this creative coping mechanism in its totality.

4. Keep silent.

For many of us chatterbox-types, this may be the

most difficult application of all. Moses tells the people at the Red Sea: "The Lord will fight for you while you keep silent."

It's hard to be quiet when we go through deep and difficult waters. Let me explain what I mean. One of the most natural reactions when going through a crisis is wanting to ask God, "Why?"

In one sense, that's what this application is all about—the motive behind the circumstance. It's not so much a restriction against conversation in general, but rather, it has a very specific focus.

The most famous story of suffering in the Bible is the story of Job. This man was put through a level of intense pain that few of us could even imagine. Interestingly enough, Job wasn't silent. He asked God why he was being asked to endure this disaster. And about forty chapters in, God finally answered, but not until Job and his "friends" had stirred His wrath with their impertinent questions and confrontations.

The prohibition is not against talking. It's not even against asking "Why?" I believe the restriction is aimed at the *attitude* behind what is said.

It's one thing to ask "Why?" with the genuine sincerity of a seeker of truth. But it's quite another issue to ask "Why?" and have behind it an attitude of, "Boy, God, You really screwed up this time! If I were in charge of my own life, I can guarantee You, a disaster of this magnitude would have never happened! What's wrong with You up there? Don't You see how messed up everything is now? If this is the way it's going to work, I think I'd prefer to run my own life!"

It is that attitude that Moses warned against. It goes back to what we discussed in Chapter 5 . . . *control.* We don't like the way God allowed circumstances to come in and redirect our lives because it was something out of our control. Well, we want control, so in our anger we yell at God and threaten to take His control away from Him, as if we could do that.

I have a friend who has gone through his share of grief and pain. He shared with me one time about a period in his life when he was living alone. Each night as he prepared for bed, he turned down his bedcovers, shut off the bedroom light, and opened the drapes to his large window. As he climbed into bed, he was perfectly situated to see the moon shining through the panes of glass. He stared out that window at the moon for hours at a time, until sleep finally arrived.

"I know this isn't theologically correct," he later told me, "but I used to imagine that God lived on the moon. Each night before I fell asleep, I would look up at the moon, shake my fist at it, and say, 'God, how could You have done this to me? My life is a total mess and it's all Your fault.'"

Then my friend would say every foul, blasphemous word he could think of. He was in an extremely bitter time in his life, and he chose to vent his emotions by swearing at God, who was conveniently living on the moon. It is this type of exercise that Moses is telling us to avoid. There just isn't any profit in it.

This point always reminds me of an old joke. The joke goes that there was this guy who always wanted to speak to God and have Him verbally respond from heaven. So, God, in His loving graciousness, grants this guy his request. "You may ask Me three questions, and I will answer you from My throne here in heaven."

The guy is all excited about finally having his wish come true. He measures his words carefully and asks his first question:

"God, is it true that a million years to You is just like a second?"

God replied, "Yes, that is true. Since I am eternal, I am not bound by the dimensions of time."

"Okay, then here's the second question," the guy continues. "Would it be true then that a million dollars to You is just like a penny?"

"That is true," God answered.

"Great. Then I have one last question. God . . . can I have a penny?"

And God said, "Yes . . . just a second."

I love that joke because it so aptly describes the human condition. We honestly believe we can corner God. We think we can get Him to fall for the old "penny equals a million dollars" scam.

But God is not a senile great-grandfather just wait-

BILL BUTTERWORTH

ing for a human to outsmart Him. He is God. He knows what is best for us, even when we can't see past the pain of the present moment. As we learn to trust Him, which is what this prescription from Moses is all about, we come to understand more about God's purposes for us here on earth. We will be asked to endure suffering, but there will always be purpose in it. Look at what God taught the children of Israel that day in the wilderness.

MIRACLES

What God did that day at the Red Sea still leaves me with chills. Here are the words recorded in Exodus:

And the angel of God, who had been going before the camp of Israel, moved and went behind them; and the pillar of cloud moved from before them and stood
behind them. So it came between the camp of Egypt and the camp of Israel; and there was the cloud along with the darkness, yet it gave light at night. Thus the one did not come near the other all night.

Then Moses stretched out his hand over the sea; and the LORD swept the sea back by a strong east wind all night, and turned the sea into dry land, so the waters were divided.[11]

God surrounded them and then miraculously parted the Red Sea! How did He do it? It's a miracle!

"And the sons of Israel went through the midst of the sea on the dry ground, and the waters were like a wall to them on their right hand and on their left."[12]

I've heard a suggestion about how this miracle could happen; some think that the phrase "the waters were like a wall" implies that the waters *congealed* the way gelatin does. I don't know if that is true or not, but it conjures up such a glorious picture. Could you imagine two million kids' total delight as the Red Sea turned into strawberry Jell-O? They would be slapping at it and plunging their arms into it only to pull them out again with a loud *schwop* as the Jell-O recongealed. This is just too much fun for former slaves to be experiencing!

Once the three million six hundred thousand Israelites were safely on the other side of the Red Sea, with the Egyptian army right behind them, God had one more use for this miracle up His divine sleeve:

> So Moses stretched out his hand over the sea, and the sea returned to its normal state at daybreak, while the Egyptians were fleeing right into it; then the LORD overthrew the Egyptians in the midst of the sea.

> And the waters returned and covered the chariots and the horsemen, even Pharaoh's entire army that had gone into the sea after them; not even one of them remained.[13]

When God allowed the waters to return to their

normal position, the Egyptian army was in the middle of them! So, in the confusion that ensued, the Egyptians were either drowned or destroyed themselves in the panic. It was truly an all-purpose miracle God had provided for His people.

Critics love to poke holes in the authenticity of this biblical account. The Red Sea is really the Reed Sea, they argue. God's parting of the water was probably only a strong wind that blew back a shallow body of water only a few inches deep, so it's no big deal, they erroneously conclude.

There is a miracle here one way or another. Either you have God miraculously parting a large body of water (which is what I believe) or else you have a highly trained, finely tuned army destroying itself in a few inches of water!

MOTIVATION

When my disappointing circumstance is reduced to its most basic form, I am left with two choices in response to it.

The first is the *natural response*: to avoid God, which keeps me from learning why God allowed the circumstance and crushes any joy I had in my inner spiritual life.

If I charted the natural response, it would look like this:

MAN   **(CIRCUMSTANCE)**   **GOD**

The other choice is the *supernatural response*. It is understanding that God has something for me to learn through all this, so I cling to Him for encouragement, support, motivation, and understanding while going through this crisis.

The supernatural response would be charted this way:

MAN   **(GOD)**   **CIRCUMSTANCE**

God is not only my buffer, but He is the one who will bring the ultimate meaning out of this disappointment in my life.

Many people grow distant from the Lord during crisis, but many others, like myself, actually draw closer to Him in the season of pain. I know that the ultimate healing of my soul is the direct act of God in my life. There have been countless pictures of His grace that seem miraculous to observe today.

I'm learning that when life doesn't turn out like you planned, it's time to turn to the Lord.

Replace the disappointment in life with the hope He always meant for you to have.

Graduation Day

It is Friday evening, June 9, 1995. Another gorgeous spring day is coming to a close in the foothills of the Sierra Nevada mountains. Our little Northern California town of Grass Valley is all abuzz with excitement and anticipation as several hundred of its teenagers will shortly be marching down an aisle created in the center of the football field to receive their high-school diplomas.

It's Graduation Day. The ceremony is to start at seven o'clock, but, like many of the other parents, I am already in my seat shortly before 5:30 P.M. My oldest child, my only daughter, Joy, is about to graduate, and I am determined that I will not be sentenced to the back of the bleachers behind the large lady with the huge hat. Arriving early pays off. I'm located in the fifth row, toward the center. My camera sits poised next to me, serving double-duty tonight by saving the seat next to me and later, taking photographs to record this event for posterity.

I sit in silent disbelief that my daughter is already old enough to be a high-school graduate. The commencement speaker will allude to this point, and it causes my mind to flood back to one particular vignette in her growing-up years: It's the summer of 1978 and I'm observing a two-year-old tomboy, whose hair is always disheveled and face is always dirty. But her smile could melt an iceberg from three hundred yards away. I remember having to yell at her for an act of misbehavior. I would point my index finger at her tiny face and say, "No, Joy! No!"

It is such a distinct memory because I can still see her going out the back door and finding a hill of ants in the backyard. Instinctively, she crouched down low to the ground, as only toddlers can do, put her face inches from the ants, pointed her index finger at them, and screamed defiantly, "No, Buggy! No."

But two years old is now eighteen years old and the dirty, disheveled toddler is now six feet tall, blonde, beautiful, and never more radiant than tonight. I am trying hard to fulfill my promise. Joy and I had a wonderfully quiet moment together earlier this afternoon, where I gave her a card, a gift, and an eight-page letter of private thoughts; then I hugged her, kissed her, and we wept together for a long time. "Dad, we can't cry tonight at graduation," she stated. "Promise me you won't cry tonight. If I see you crying, I'll burst into tears, so you have to be strong, okay? Do you promise?"

Seeing Joy at graduation, with my four sons seated on my right and on my left, I am overwhelmed at how God has seen us through the most difficult time in our lives. It seems fitting that I am having these thoughts at graduation, for school officials have always referred to graduation as *commencement*, meaning that the emphasis is not on what has been completed, but that the rest of life is just beginning.

Earlier that week, as Joy prepared for graduation, among the reams of papers that we received to clarify all that must be accomplished, one form caught my attention. It was called the Year-End Activities Check-Out form. This sheet of paper contained a list of functions that all seniors must *clear* before they will be able to participate in Friday night's ceremony. It included things like:

- Turn in all your textbooks.
- Return all your library books.
- Pay all overdue library book fees.
- Turn in all athletic equipment.
- Pay all school-parking fines.
- Get form signed by academic adviser signifying completion of all academic units.
- Turn in all completed forms for *clearance*.

It was that word *clearance* that continually jumped off the page at me. Even in reading a simple checklist for prospective graduates, I learned a lesson. The school was creating a basic policy that stated: *You cannot move on in life* (graduation ceremony) *until you clear up all that's behind you from the previous year.*

As a Christian, I understood what this meant in the broader perspective. It was pointing to the necessary issue that brings closure to crisis . . . *forgiveness.*

As I sat in the stadium, watching the sun slowly hide behind the western hills, I thought about forgiveness. I realized how important it had been in my healing to be able to ask my kids to forgive me for my shortcomings—especially the ones that had surfaced in the last two years. I realized how vital it was for me to ask Rhonda for her forgiveness and how much it meant to me that she quickly consented. I have forgiven her, as well, and that has released me from the cuffs and chains that imprison anyone unable to come to that point.

Without forgiveness there is bitterness. It is axiomatic. Bitterness is the stuff of stomach ulcers, unending headaches, and nausea. It's the plague of the person who can only utter, "I just can't seem to get over it. I just can't let it go."

Ultimate healing will not take place until forgiveness is achieved.

Don't misunderstand, forgiving is very different from forgetting. Every day is a reminder of what used to be, but because of forgiveness it is not as debilitating as it once was. I am doing much better than I was doing two years ago. This book is solid evidence of that fact. I am in a better position to *commence* the rest of my life because I have sought to achieve *clearance* from that which is behind me.

The seniors are lined up, ready to march. I am in perfect position for what is about to happen. I have my camera up to my eye, and I am still wearing my sunglasses, even though they are unnecessary in the dusk. As the administrator reads aloud the name, "Joy Lynn Butterworth," I snap three or four shots as she accepts her diploma, shakes the principal's hand, and marches off the platform. Fortunately, behind the camera and sunglasses, my tears are not evident even as they stream down my cheeks. I guess it doesn't really matter, though, for Joy is in the same river of tears without any inducement from me.

It is one of those all-purpose cries:

Tears of sadness.

Tears of joy.

Tears of love.

Tears of fear.

Tears of gratitude to God.

Tears of clearance.

Tears of commencement.

NOTES

Chapter 2

1. Philippians 4:11.

Chapter 3

1. Psalm 46:10 (KJV).

Chapter 4

1. "Count Your Blessings," copyright 1925, by E. J. Excell, Hope Publishing Company.

Chapter 5

1. Jeremiah 18:1–10.
2. Jeremiah 19:1–4, 8, 10–11.
3. Isaiah 30:13–15.
4. Andy Andrews, Storms of Perfection (Murfreesboro, TN: Lightning Crown, 1992).

Chapter 6

1. Norman Wright, *Recovering from the Losses of Life* (Grand Rapids: Revell, 1993), 45-46.
2. Ibid.
3. Stephen Covey, *The Seven Habits of Highly Effective People,* (New York: S&S Trade, 1989).
4. Philippians 3:10.

Chapter 7
1. Luke 4:18.
2. Isaiah 61:1.

Chapter 8
1. Proverbs 23:7.

Chapter 11
1. Exodus 5:1–2.
2. Exodus 11:7.
3. Exodus 12:30.
4. Exodus 12:31.
5. Exodus 12:37.
6. Exodus 14:5–7.
7. Exodus 14:10–12.
8. Philip Yancey, *Where Is God When It Hurts?* (Grand Rapids: Zondervan, 1977), 140.
9. Proverbs 12:25.
10. Leon Wood, *A Survey of Israel's History* (Grand Rapids: Zondervan, 1970), 134–35.
11. Exodus 14:19–21.
12. Exodus 14:22.
13. Exodus 14:27–28.